KAY ARTHUR

Return to the
Garden

EMBRACING GOD'S DESIGN FOR
SEXUALITY

LifeWay Press®
Nashville, Tennessee

Published by LifeWay Press®

© 2008 Kay Arthur

No part of this book may be reproduced or transmitted in any form or by any means,
electronic or mechanical, including photocopying and recording, or by any information storage
or retrieval system, except as may be expressly permitted in writing by the publisher.
Requests for permission should be addressed in writing to
LifeWay Press®; One LifeWay Plaza; Nashville, TN 37234-0175.

ISBN 141585291

Item 005146923

This book is the resource for course CG-1330 in the subject area
Bible Studies in the Christian Growth Study Plan.
Dewey Decimal classification: 176
Subject Headings: SEXUAL ETHICS \ SEXUAL BEHAVIOR \
WOMEN—SEXUAL BEHAVIOR

Material in this resource is adapted from *The Truth about Sex: What the World Won't Tell You
and God Wants You to Know* © 2005 by Kay Arthur. Published by Waterbrook Press;
Eugene, Oregon 97402. Used by permission.

Unless otherwise noted, all biblical quotations are from the New American Standard Bible®,
Copyright © 1960, 1962, 1963, 1968, 1971, 1972, 1973, 1975, 1977, 1995 by
The Lockman Foundation, Used by permission. *(www.lockman.org)*
Scriptures marked NIV are from the Holy Bible, New International Version,
copyright © 1973, 1978, 1984 by International Bible Society.

To order additional copies of this resource: write to LifeWay Church Resources Customer
Service; One LifeWay Plaza; Nashville, TN 37234-0013; fax (615) 251-5933;
phone toll free (800) 458-2772; order online at *www.lifeway.com;* e-mail *orderentry@lifeway.com;*
or visit the LifeWay Christian Store serving you.

Printed in the United States of America

Leadership and Adult Publishing
LifeWay Church Resources
One LifeWay Plaza
Nashville, TN 37234-0175

Contents

ABOUT THE *Author*

In the late 1960s, a missionary couple in Mexico suffered medical problems and returned home to Chattanooga. Little did they know that God had a greater field of ministry for them. Jack Arthur became station manager for a Christian radio station, and Kay Arthur started a Bible study for teenagers in their living room. By 1970 youth were meeting in a barn they had cleaned out and patched up themselves. Soon adults were coming too.

The first women's Bible study class began, and the word spread. Night classes started. Soon Kay was traveling to Atlanta, Georgia, every week to teach nearly 1,800 adults. Knowing she and Jack would not be able to travel every week, Kay wanted to teach others to study inductively and so began writing Precept Upon Precept courses.

Jack left his radio career and became president and leader of this flourishing new organization. Today Precept Ministries International (*www.precept.org*) reaches into 150 countries with studies in 70 languages for children, teens, and adults.

Through the many ministries of Precept—including the daily radio and television program "Precepts for Life," Kay Arthur has touched millions of lives. A well-known conference speaker and author, Kay has a unique ability to reach people in an exciting, effective way—teaching them how to discover truth for themselves so truth can change their lives and equip them to be used to advance God's kingdom.

Amy Summers, an experienced writer for LifeWay adult Bible study and discipleship resources, wrote the leader guide. Amy is a wife, mother, and Sunday School leader living in Arden, North Carolina. She is a graduate of Baylor University and Southwestern Baptist Theological Seminary.

Discovering God's truth for *Yourself*

Inductive study, a method that bring you directly to the Word of God apart from another person's understanding or interpretation of the text, involves three skills: *observation, interpretation,* and *application.*

Observation teaches you to see precisely what the passage says. Observation answers the question: What does the passage say? **Interpretation** answers the question: What does the passage mean? **Application** answers the questions: What truths can I put into practice? What changes should I make in my life, in my beliefs, in my thinking? When you know what God says and means, and put His truths into practice, you will be equipped for every circumstance of life.

Never forget that it is the indwelling Holy Spirit who takes the things of God and reveals them to us. Always ask God to teach you as you open the Scriptures, which is His Word to you.

OBSERVATION: WHAT DOES THE PASSAGE SAY?

Kay will lead you in this study of sexuality to look at Scripture and to ask the questions *Who? What? When? Where? Why?* and *How?* Accurate answers to these questions will help you stay true to the context of a passage and ensure correct interpretation. Don't be concerned if you cannot find the answers to all of the questions every time. As you ask *what, when, who, where, why,* and *how,* make notes in the margin of your Bible. Meditate on the truths God reveals to you and think how they apply to you.

A **key word** is considered essential to the text; when it is removed, the passage is devoid of meaning. Often key words are repeated to convey the biblical author's point or purpose in writing. They may be repeated throughout a chapter, a segment of a book, or the book as a whole. Kay will help you learn to mark key words.

Then as you list what you learn from marking a key word, ask the same *who, what, when, where, why,* and *how* questions as you did for passages of Scripture. For example, if you are marking the word *suffering,* then note *Who* suffered? *What* caused the suffering? and so forth.

Key words can be marked in several ways: through symbols, colors, or a combination of symbols and colors. When you mark key words, mark synonyms and pronouns just as you mark the words to which they refer. Always mark each key word the same way each time you observe it. In future Bible study, the visual impact of your marks will help you track key subjects and quickly identify significant truths throughout Scripture. You will see this as you go through this study with Kay.

INTERPRETATION: WHAT DOES THE PASSAGE MEAN?

While observation leads to an accurate understanding of what the Word of God *says,* interpretation goes a step further and help you understand what it *means.* When you learn to accurately interpret the Word of God, you will be able to confidently put its truths into practice in your daily life. Certain principles are part of this important process:

- Always know that context rules
- Always seek the full counsel of the Word of God
- Be aware that Scripture will never contradict Scripture
- Don't base your convictions on an obscure passage
- Interpret Scripture literally
- Always try to understand what the biblical author had in mind when you interpret a portion of Scripture.

APPLICATION: WHAT TRUTHS CAN I PUT INTO PRACTICE?

In applying Scripture to your life, ask yourself these questions: *What does the passage teach? Does this section of Scripture expose any error in my beliefs or behavior? What is God's instruction to me as His child?*

No matter how much you know about God's Word, if you don't apply what you learn, Scripture will never benefit your life. Transformation is the goal of any study of God's Word.

ABOUT THIS Study

"O, precious one, there is so much I would love to teach you about purity, about marriage, about covenant, about studying the Bible. I don't know where you are or where you have been in your sexuality; but I do know the Father's heart for His daughter, and I can tell you it is good, so good that you cannot comprehend it."

—Kay Arthur, *Return to the Garden*

And teach she does in *Return to the Garden: Embracing God's Design for Sexuality.* Bible teacher Kay Arthur points women to God's Word for *His* truth and design for sexuality, challenging them to stand strong. This six-session Bible study, updated from Kay's *The Truth About Sex,* will help married women make appropriate commitments to God and to their husbands and single women accomplish God's purpose for them in their singleness.

Return to the Garden provides a safe time and place to talk about a deeply personal subject. Home study guides women to discover what God has to say and to respond to Him as they study the Bible for themselves. Group sessions are enhanced by Kay's strong biblical teaching on DVD and by the insights of a caring small group of women. Teaching suggestions (pp. 182-191) are based on 90 minutes; adapt as needed for your group.

Choose a setting that helps you accomplish your purposes for this study. *Return to the Garden* lends itself to a home study or other setting away from the church. (For a retreat schedule, go to *www.lifeway.com/women* and search "Return to the Garden.") In a day when marriages and families are so at risk, this study can be timely.

These additional resources provide support for leading the study: Leader Kit (Item 005035532); Audio CDs (Item 005147046); and online *www.lifeway.com/women.*

Viewer Guide
Session I

KNOWLEDGE OF GOD IN THE LAND

HOSEA 4:1

"_____ to the word of the LORD, O sons of Israel,
For the LORD has a case against the inhabitants of the land,
Because there is no faithfulness or kindness
Or _Knowledge_ of God in the land."

If you don't have a knowledge of God, you don't have anything
to _____ you.

HOSEA 4:6

"My people are destroyed for lack of knowledge
Because you have rejected knowledge,
I also will reject you from being My priest.
Since you have forgotten the law of your God,
I also will forget your _Children_."

I'm on a mission to help you have a _Knowledge_ of God
and look at the Word of God _____.

Change of mind results in a change of _Mind_.

It is your calling as a _Child (daughter)_ of God to know the
Word of God.

who
what
when
where -
How

Color
coded

THE BEAUTY OF A WOMAN'S *Sexuality*

From beginning to end, the Bible is about a divine romance. It opens with the account of a man and a woman becoming one flesh. It ends with the Spirit and the bride inviting others to join God's forever family.

The Book of books, the Bible, opens with a wedding and a garden. So, beloved, we want to begin there, too. I'm glad we're on this journey together to look at the beauty and intimacy God has always intended for our relationship with our husbands.

THIS WEEK, THROUGH YOUR
HOME STUDY, YOU WILL:

grow in your love for studying God's Word

understand the importance God places
on sexuality

learn or reaffirm God's design for creating
people uniquely male and female

discover how to live for God in a sex-saturated
culture, protecting your heart and mind from
cultural temptations

Pleasing
TO HIM

Within our society today, and even within the church, many are confused about sex and sexual morality. We see a growing movement toward accepting behaviors that were almost universally considered immoral just a few decades ago. These days, sexual innuendo and even sexual acts are flaunted on prime-time television. The attitude that sex is a form of entertainment, a harmless and meaningless interaction between two consenting people, has seeped into every aspect of our culture.

Why does our culture seem to be obsessed with sexuality? Is sex, as current trends would seem to indicate, simply a bodily function, as instinctual and irresistible as the need to satisfy our hunger and thirst? Or is there something holy and beautiful about sex, something we are missing, something we should treasure? These are critical questions for us to think about and answer both as a society and as individuals.

How important do *you* think it is for us as women to understand our sexuality? Don't you need and want to know, as I do . . .

- Why you are woman, uniquely designed by God and designed to fit with man—designed to satisfy your husband, enjoy his physical nearness, and bear and nurture the children who are born as a result of such a time of intimacy?
- If you are called by God to remain single—what does this mean? You may be asking yourself, *How am I to handle my sexuality, my desires, and retain my unique femininity as I move into the world to accomplish God's purpose in my singleness?*
- How you can help your daughters understand this gift of sexuality as they mature and find themselves drawn to the opposite sex?

I have discovered that sexuality is a subject rarely addressed by the church or within the confines of the church building unless it is to condemn adultery or other sexual sins. Why? Because it just doesn't seem appropriate, does it, to discuss such an intimate subject in the context of Christianity? *God* and *sex* don't seem to belong in the same sentence! And yet, let's think this through by answering a couple of questions.

Where is our sexuality usually discussed?

By whom?

In what kind of an atmosphere?

Who invented sex? Who came up with the concept?

Were there any parameters set by the "inventor" on how we are to handle our sexuality as women?

Is there any disparity or conflict with the culture in the area of a woman's sexuality? List your observations.

That's a lot to think about it, isn't it? But I don't want you to think about it apart from the Word of God. It's the measuring rod of truth. The first passage we'll look at is Paul's first letter to the church at Thessalonica, a city in Greece. Read these verses aloud to help you focus on the text and remember it.

I THESSALONIANS 4:1-8

[1] Finally then, brethren, we request and exhort you in the Lord Jesus, that as you received from us instruction as to how you ought to walk and please God (just as you actually do walk), that you excel still more.

[2] For you know what commandments we gave you by the authority of the Lord Jesus.

[3] For this is the will of God, your sanctification; that is, that you abstain from sexual immorality;

[4] that each of you know how to possess his own vessel in sanctification and honor,

[5] not in lustful passion, like the Gentiles who do not know God;

[6] and that no man transgress and defraud his brother in the matter because the Lord is the avenger in all these things, just as we also told you before and solemnly warned you.

[7] For God has not called us for the purpose of impurity, but in sanctification.

[8] So, he who rejects this is not rejecting man but the God who gives His Holy Spirit to you.

Now read through the text again, and this time mark all the references to the recipients of Paul's letter: every *you*, *your*, *his*, and *us* (when Paul included himself with the Thessalonians). I would suggest you color-code them in a specific color, for example, orange; however, if you don't have colored pencils, you can underline them.

Now read the text again—aloud—and color every reference to God in another color. I usually color the references to Him in yellow because God is light! If you want to use a symbol instead, you might try a triangle.

When you finish, list what you learned from marking the references to recipients and what you learned from marking the references to God.

THE RECIPIENTS   GOD

Good! Summarize what you just learned from His Word about your sexuality.

How important is it?

How important, then, do you think it is that we know what God has to say about our sexuality?

God has far more to say about the subject of purity. Did you notice the phrase in I Thessalonians 4:4: "know how to possess his own vessel in sanctification and honor"? This, beloved, will be our goal in doing this study: learning how to live victoriously in an amoral, sex-saturated culture. Not shaped nor conformed to the style of the world but living life on a higher plane as a woman of God—set apart for Him. Honoring what He has given us and created us to be with a passion "to be pleasing to Him" (2 Cor. 5:9).

I guarantee that if you will make the apostle Paul's ambition yours, you will experience a deeply settled peace rather than a tortured conscience. The latter is like living in the path of a threatening storm. You never know when it will rain on your day or blow off the roof!

DISTINCTIVELY AND DELIGHTFULLY FEMALE

From the very beginning, from the sixth day of creation when God the Father, Son, and Holy Spirit made "man (mankind) in [their] image, according to [their] likeness" we've been defined as female, as woman—someone different than man, the male (Gen. 1:26). Thus, it's evident, isn't it, that from the very beginning our sexuality has been front and center with God?

But that is enough from me! As in everything, my purpose in writing this study is *you*, to help *you* discover for yourself what God says in His Book, the Bible. My passion is to get me out of the way so you can hear from God yourself and know firsthand what God said. I want you to:

- Fall in love with the Word of God and prefer it over the writings of any human.
- Long to study God's Word, and not be able to get enough!

It would be an answer to Jesus' prayer for you in John 17:15-17. His Word, beloved, is truth—and it is what sets you apart for a life that is pleasing to Him.

With all that said, let's turn to the first chapter of the first book of the Bible, to Genesis, which means *beginnings*. As you read Genesis 1:25-28, color-code every reference to "man," including every pronoun (every *him*, every *them*) and synonym (such as *male*). Then in a different color, mark the references to the woman. If you use colors, mark man in blue and woman in pink. (If you use symbols, then use these ♂♀ for male and female.)

GENESIS 1:25-28

25 God made the beasts of the earth after their kind, and the cattle after their kind, and everything that creeps on the ground after its kind; and God saw that it was good.

26 Then God said, "Let Us make man in Our image, according to Our likeness; and let them rule over the fish of the sea and over the birds of the sky and over the cattle and over all the earth, and over every creeping thing that creeps on the earth."

27 God created man in His own image, in the image of God He created him; male and female He created them.

28 God blessed them; and God said to them, "Be fruitful and multiply, and fill the earth, and subdue it; and rule over the fish of the sea and over the birds of the sky and over every living thing that moves on the earth."

Before we analyze what we've seen, let's look at Genesis 2, where God tightened the focus on the telescope and takes us in for a closer look at the details of His creation of man and woman. As you read, continue marking all the references to the man and all the references to the woman. What you are doing is approaching the text *inductively:* going straight to the Word of God and observing what it says.

GENESIS 2:7-8,15-25

7 Then the LORD God formed man of dust from the ground, and breathed into his nostrils the breath of life; and man became a living being.

8 The LORD God planted a garden toward the east, in Eden; and there He placed the man whom He had formed. ...

15 Then the LORD God took the man and put him into the garden of Eden to cultivate it and keep it.

16 The LORD God commanded the man, saying, "From any tree of the garden you may eat freely;

17 but from the tree of the knowledge of good and evil you shall not eat, for in the day that you eat from it you will surely die."

¹⁸ Then the Lord God said, "It is not good for the man to be alone; I will make him a helper suitable for him."

¹⁹ Out of the ground the Lord God formed every beast of the field and every bird of the sky, and brought them to the man to see what he would call them; and whatever the man called a living creature, that was its name.

²⁰ The man gave names to all the cattle, and to the birds of the sky, and to every beast of the field, but for Adam there was not found a helper suitable for him.

²¹ So the Lord God caused a deep sleep to fall upon the man, and he slept; then He took one of his ribs and closed up the flesh at that place.

²² The Lord God fashioned into a woman the rib which He had taken from the man, and brought her to the man.

²³ The man said, "This is now bone of my bones, And flesh of my flesh; She shall be called Woman, Because she was taken out of Man."

²⁴ For this reason a man shall leave his father and his mother, and be joined to his wife; and they shall become one flesh.

²⁵ And the man and his wife were both naked and were not ashamed.

Now list what you learned from marking Genesis 1 and 2.

MAN   WOMAN

In Genesis 2 God not only showed us the order of creation—man and then the woman—but He also told us why woman was created.

What did you observe about the reason for her creation?

Now read the text again and underline the phrase "a helper suitable." It is used more than once.

While Adam was created from the dust of the earth, the woman was created from a rib taken from the side of a man and brought to man to be his *ezer neged*. A helper suitable! *Ezer* means "an aide, an assistant" while *neged* means "a counterpart." The man's helper was not another man but a counterpart! "Prominently before, usually superior at points of difference and infrequently inferior."[1]

That ought to be an encouragement, dear sisters! Distinctively and delightfully female! Adam was pleased with God's gift!

Since our sexuality as women is the thrust of our study, let me give you one more truth from God's Word and we'll call it a day: Genesis 1 tells us that both man and woman were created on the sixth day, given dominion over the earth, and told to be fruitful and multiply and fill the earth (1:28-31).

What would it take to fulfill that command? I don't mean to be a dork in asking that question, and if you're sitting with your daughter and she's throwing up her hands saying, "Mom! We can't talk about this!" just look at her and remind her that she is sitting there as your daughter because ... The reason is in the answer.

Write out what you learned in Genesis 1:28.

Designer
GOODS

A picture remains in my mind, one that I will never forget. When I was 12 years old, I was doing my homework while listening to the radio. I loved listening to the radio and had every program time memorized. One of the programs I loved to listen to was a science program. Mother was a nurse, as was Aunt Daisy. And I wanted to be a nurse.

I loved looking through the old medical books with pictures and sketches of all sorts of fascinating anomalies—tumors with teeth and hair, heads bigger than they should have been, people with elephantiasis.

As I was sitting at the table in our two-bedroom home, the program came on. It was about the RH factor of the blood, explaining what could happen to the baby if the father and mother's blood were not compatible. Puzzled, I put my pencil down and turned toward the kitchen. "Mother, what does the father's blood have to do with the baby anyway?"

All I remember were Mother's first words, "Oh, Kay, it's so beautiful." That was my first lesson on sex!

When you think of sex, what words come to your mind?
It's important to know because our actions and responses
are a product of our thoughts. Record your words here.

When God designed us—male and female—what was in His thoughts? Was sex something of beauty to Him? Or at the least, something dirty or disgusting? Something you have to endure if you want to have babies? Did God intend for women to enjoy sex?

Are we only to discover the mysteries of our sexuality at slumber parties or at the feet of girls who have "done it" and therefore, of course, know all about it? Is it something too intimate to discuss with mothers who probably don't know anything anyway or would be *too* horrified, *too* embarrassed, or *too* unreasonable to talk to?

If you are tracking with me, I think you are beginning to see the answers to these questions. From the very beginning of time, our sexuality and distinctiveness as women has been front and center with God. We are designer goods, designed by God, no less! He made us women. And when it comes to our sexuality, He has much to say.

In Genesis 1 He told man and woman to be fruitful, multiply, and fill the earth, and He wasn't talking about doing math! This instruction repeats in Genesis 2, and that is what I want us to look at today. Remember, my mama told me it was beautiful, so beautiful. And you know what? I am sure she told me more, but that is all I can remember.

Go back to page 18 and read the Genesis 2 passage again, giving special attention to verse 24. Many wonderful truths in this passage give us great insight into marriage, but for now at least, we are going to pass over them. (If you want to study them ... and you need to if you are married or contemplating marriage ... we have an incredible Precept Upon Precept course, as well as an In & Out study on *A Marriage Without Regrets*. I mention other tools in the footnote.)[2]

Now write out Genesis 2:24 in this space.

"Become one flesh." What does that mean? The best interpreter of God is God; therefore, the best interpreter of Scripture is Scripture since all Scripture is "God breathed." As Jesus quoted from Deuteronomy, "Man shall not live on bread alone, but on every word that proceeds out of the mouth of God" (Matt. 4:4). Did you get it as well as read it? Jesus just said the Bible comes from the mouth of God! According to Jesus and according to 2 Timothy 3:16-17 and 2 Peter 1:21, the Bible is comprised of one thing: the very words of God! Oh, beloved, why do we prefer the words of mankind above, over, or against the words of Yahweh—the Almighty, self-existent God?

Now, let's get God's word on "one flesh." It is in Paul's letter to the church at Corinth. A chief city in Greece, Corinth overlooked a narrow isthmus that connected the Greek mainland with Peloponnesus, thus receiving ships and their sailors from two corners of the world. It was a very cosmopolitan city inundated with people who worshiped all sorts of idols and embraced a variety of philosophies. With its temple to Aphrodite, the goddess of love, who touted no moral standards, Corinth was a hotbed of a thousand temple prostitutes plying their wares seemingly without condemnation.

Then came Paul with the gospel of Christianity—naming sin as sin, promising forgiveness from the one and only true God, and calling people to righteousness that comes by faith in Jesus Christ alone. To those who believed and received Jesus as the Son of God and therefore their Lord and Master, he wrote the following words.

Read Paul's words aloud.

I CORINTHIANS 6:15-20

¹⁵ Do you not know that your bodies are members of Christ? Shall I then take away the members of Christ and make them members of a prostitute? May it never be!

¹⁶ Or do you not know that the one who joins himself to a prostitute is one body with her? For He says, "THE TWO SHALL BECOME ONE FLESH."

¹⁷ But the one who joins himself to the Lord is one spirit with Him.

¹⁸ Flee immorality. Every other sin that a man commits is outside the body, but the immoral man sins against his own body.

¹⁹ Or do you not know that your body is a temple of the Holy
    Spirit who is in you, whom you have from God, and that
    you are not your own?
²⁰ For you have been bought with a price: therefore glorify
    God in your body.

Now read this passage again, but this time draw a stick
figure like this 🧍 over every reference to the body, including
the synonymous term "members of Christ." Now list what
you learned from marking the references to the body—
any part.

Now, beloved of God, according to I Corinthians,
considering the context of this passage and remembering
that context rules over interpretation, what did God mean
when He spoke that "THE TWO SHALL BECOME ONE FLESH"?
Two who? Two when?

So is sex as we call it today part of God's design?
○ Yes ○ No Why or why not?

When you think how God designed us anatomically as man and woman—
in the act of marriage, man fits right into woman, thus truly, physically,
making them one flesh! It is beautiful, isn't it—if it's God's way?

  Think about what you've seen for yourself in God's Word; then
tomorrow we'll talk more about it.

THE BEAUTY GOD
INTENDS

It's so incredible, so awesome. Becoming one flesh is what sex is by God's design. When God made Adam and Eve distinctively male and female, He designed them anatomically so they could physically become one flesh in the act of sexual intercourse.

God formed us to know no greater ecstasy than when a man and a woman literally merge into one flesh. Hormones, nerves, sensory receptors, and other specific physical characteristics are all part of His divine design for our pleasure. An ecstasy beyond exquisite. A oneness washing over you, a wave of passion carrying you weightless to a sea of delight. Passion that loses consciousness of anything else. Exhaustion that leaves you spent, drained of tension and filled with satisfaction, total satisfaction. Spent—and able to rest.

Sex has a beauty all its own and—wonder of wonders—God invented it!

Do you realize that God didn't have to make sex so pleasurable? He simply could have given the instructions: "In order to be fruitful and multiply first do this, then that, and follow with this. Be careful of such and such. Hopefully nine months later you will produce a child. If there are no indicators that the process has worked, repeat again until successful." No feelings, no passion, no exhilaration—just mechanics!

But God designed sex to be more than just mechanical; it's to be deeply satisfying, comfortable, fulfilling, and at times very passionate. True intimacy involves not only truly belonging to another but also being comfortable and secure, free from performance, and knowing a oneness that you have with no other until death parts you. It is to be pure, holy, and free from condemnation and guilt.

This, beloved, is what God intends sex to be. We'll study it more later, but know this—if guilt is written all over your sexuality, you can experience forgiveness, restoration, and purity. But for now ...

HIS COVENANT RELATIONSHIP AND A DIVINE ROMANCE

Have you ever thought how God used the marriage of the very first man and woman, their oneness, as an illustration of the faithfulness and oneness He desired with His chosen people Israel, to whom He referred as His wife? He used His Son's union with His bride, the church, as an example of how a husband and wife should relate to one another.

From beginning to end, the Bible is about a divine romance. It opens with the account of a man and woman becoming one flesh. It ends with the Holy Spirit and the bride inviting others to join God's forever family. The Old Testament shows us the joy of fidelity and the heart-wrenching pain of adultery. We watch as God took the canvas of the Old Testament and painted the picture of His love affair with Israel—all on the basis of an everlasting covenant: a solemn binding agreement to fulfill His oath to His chosen people, a people chosen above all other nations.

In Ezekiel 16 God sketched the picture of Israel's birth, abandoned in a field, her little body unwashed, squirming in her blood, her cord uncut. Our hearts are touched as we observe His care, raising her as His own until it was the time of love. For a moment God paused, a smile crossed His face as He remembered through Jeremiah the prophet the devotion of her youth, the love of their betrothal, the way she followed Him through the wilderness (see Jer. 2). Then the day came: " 'I passed by you and saw you, and behold, you were at the time for love; so I spread My skirt over you and covered your nakedness. I also swore to you and entered into a covenant with you so that you became Mine,' declares the Lord GOD" (Ezek. 16:8).

A covenant is a solemn binding agreement between two parties, whether lesser and greater or of equal status, who commit themselves to each other under certain conditions. Once a covenant is made, it is never to be broken. In a covenant relationship two become one and no longer live independently of one another. They are now bound to protect and defend one another, share everything in common—no more *yours* and *mine* but rather *ours*. Each party is to be there for the other until death.

Such agreements are so solemn that God becomes the sovereign administrator of every covenant—watching to make certain its conditions are fulfilled. He not only comes to the defense of the violated one, but He also deals retribution against the violator. Pause and see what the prophet Malachi, whose name means "messenger," said about marriage—and why God was not responding to His people.

First read the passage aloud and then mark the text.

MALACHI 2:13-16

13 "This is another thing you do: you cover the altar of the LORD with tears, with weeping and with groaning, because He no longer regards the offering or accepts it with favor from your hand.

14 "Yet you say, 'For what reason?' Because the LORD has been a witness between you and the wife of your youth, against whom you have dealt treacherously, though she is your companion and your wife by covenant.

15 "But not one has done so who has a remnant of the Spirit. And what did that one do while he was seeking a godly offspring? Take heed then to your spirit, and let no one deal treacherously against the wife of your youth.

16 "For I hate divorce," says the LORD, the God of Israel, "and him who covers his garment with wrong," says the LORD of hosts. "So take heed to your spirit, that you do not deal treacherously."

Now read it again. This time color-code references to *you* in orange, for instance, and all the references to the LORD *(God)*, **including pronouns, in yellow or with a yellow triangle.**

When you finish, list what you learn from marking *you* and what you learn from marking references to the LORD.

       YOU   THE LORD

A LIFE-CHANGING COVENANT

Whenever I come across the word *covenant* in my Bible, I always color-code it because everything God does is based on covenant. The New Testament word for *covenant* is *testament.* Thus the Bible has two main divisions: the Old Testament (covenant) and the New Testament (covenant). I color the word *testament* red and then box it in yellow. Why red? Because the words *made a covenant* mean "cut a covenant."[3]

Genesis 15 tells us that when God made (cut) a covenant with Abraham, the blood of animals was shed. Exodus 24 records that when the children of Israel entered into the covenant of the Law, again animals' blood was shed. In the New Testament, Jesus spoke of the covenant in His blood.

Mark the word *covenant* in the segment you just read from Malachi. Then write out what you learned from marking it. When you look at words you mark in the text, it is always good to ask the five W's and an H: *Who, what, when, where, why,* and *how* and see how many are answered in that text.

For instance, who made the covenant? With whom?

What kind of a covenant was it?

When was it made? **When** was it being talked about?

Was **where** mentioned? **Why** the response? **How** was it happening?

O, precious lady, I would love to teach you so much about marriage, about covenant … about studying the Bible, but this is enough for today. I want you to bring today to a close in prayer. I don't know where you are or where you have been in your sexuality. But I know what your Creator wants you to know: What His Father's heart has for you as His daughter, or daughter-to-be, is good—so good you cannot comprehend it.

Voice your thoughts, fears, and frustrations, your prayer to the only One who is God and the only One who can truly meet all your needs.

DAY FIVE

HOLY TO THE
LORD

Let's go back to God's love for His covenant nation, Israel, which He likened to marriage, and then we'll get to you because you can learn much from God's dealings with Israel.

Nothing was too good for His wife. He adorned her with ornaments, putting bracelets on her hand, a necklace around her neck, and a beautiful crown upon her head. Her dresses were of fine linen, silk, and embroidered cloth. She ate the choicest foods. Exceedingly beautiful, she advanced to royalty. Ezekiel 16 tells us all about how God bestowed His splendor on her and her fame spread. Then it happened.

Israel trusted in her beauty and began to play the harlot, pouring out her favors on every passerby. She sacrificed their children on the altars of fame and fortune. What was once beauty became lewdness. Many experienced her nakedness: "You . . . made your beauty abominable, and you spread your legs to every passer-by," and God's heart broke (Ezek. 16:25).

Eventually, to get her attention, He wrote her a bill of divorcement and sent her away (Jer. 3:8)—but she was never far from his heart. She descended into greater degradation until she ended up for sale in a slave market where God went to redeem His beloved Israel. The story of Hosea and Gomer gives us the picture of His redemptive love—yet again in the context of marriage (Hos. 1–3).

Israel's redemption would come through their own son, Jesus, the promised seed of Abraham, the son of David, born of the virgin as prophesied (Isa. 7:14; 9:6). He who knew no sin would become sin for us that He might save His people from their sins (2 Cor. 5:20-21).

In the fullness of time, God sought a bride for their son. The bride, a half-breed Jew and Gentile slave of sin, was offered in the slave market at a terrible price (Gal. 3:16; Eph. 2–3; 1 Pet. 1:18). Yet the Father and Son did not hesitate to pay. They counseled together to redeem her with the blood of her betrothed.

The covenant of marriage has been cut at Calvary, but the marriage has not yet been consummated. Jesus is at His Father's house preparing a place for His bride, the church. The Father's servants are watching over her, urging her to stay pure so that she might be presented as a chaste virgin when the trumpet sounds and with shouts of joy He at last will come to take her home. Longing and looking for that day, she is preparing her bridal gown, white and clean, as the invitations go out to the marriage supper of the Lamb (Rev. 19:6-9).[4]

The Book of books, the Bible, opens with a wedding and a home in the garden of Eden, then closes with a wedding and the new Jerusalem coming down out of heaven from God, made ready as a bride adorned for her husband (see Gen. 2; Rev. 21). And what do we find near the middle of this Book of books, the Bible? We find the Song of Songs, the greatest of all love songs ever written, the Song of Solomon—a song that from beginning to end extols the beauty of expressing our God-given sexuality with our spouse. A story of unquenchable, priceless love, a love that so satisfies our deepest longings that we turn to no other for we know that "I am my beloved's and my beloved is mine ... And his desire is for me" (Song of Solomon 6:3; 7:10).

It is a book that does not mention God, nor does it need to, for it is the very expression of all God intended when He made us male and female and brought woman to man. A book that cautions us not to arouse or awaken love until it pleases ... lest we mar its intended beauty and unique intimacy. Wasn't Paul referring to this in his letter to the Corinthians? After all, this is a letter dictated by God from His heart.

Let's return there for a moment and hear God's warning, His reminder of who we are, of whose we are.

Read the verses again printed out below. This time color-code or underline every *you*, *your*, *I*, and *the one*. As you do, beloved, know this is *God* speaking these truths to you ...

I CORINTHIANS 6:15-20

15 Do you not know that your bodies are members of Christ? Shall I then take away the members of Christ and make them members of a prostitute? May it never be!

16 Or do you not know that the one who joins himself to a prostitute is one body with her? For He says, "THE TWO SHALL BECOME ONE FLESH."

17 But the one who joins himself to the Lord is one spirit with Him.

18 Flee immorality. Every other sin that a man commits is outside the body, but the immoral man sins against his own body.

19 Or do you not know that your body is a temple of the Holy Spirit who is in you, whom you have from God, and that you are not your own?

20 For you have been bought with a price: therefore glorify God in your body.

To whom was God speaking through the apostle Paul—believers or nonbelievers? How do you know from the text?

• Of what was He reminding them? (Look at the places you marked and see what you learn.)

• What are you to flee and why?

• I know you saw this earlier, but what is your body? Who owns the members of your body?

• How were they "owned"? Who purchased them and at what price?

Now, take a good look, beloved, at your body—what are you doing with His eyes, His ears, His mouth, His arms, His legs, the parts of His body that are designed for sexual delight and expression only with a covenant partner, your husband—and no one else?

• How do you dress His body? What message does it give?

• Is everything in His temple saying "Holy to the Lord"?

What do you need to do in light of what you have learned this week?

And finally, precious lady, what is your prayer? Are you sure you are His child? Does your changed life prove it as 2 Corinthians 5:17 says?

If not, I have shared with you that you become a child of God when you believe—in your heart, not just your head—that Jesus is the promised One from God, the Messiah, the Christ, the Son of God—without sin, God in the flesh. He is the One who paid for all your sins, was made sin for you, and consequently who died because of your sin, who was buried but who rose from the dead never to die again. When you believe that and receive Jesus, then you are born again by His Spirit and are a child of God.

If you are not a child of God and want to become one, write in your own handwriting "I do." Record the date and watch for the changes that will come because now His Spirit resides within.

_____ Date: _____

And, by the way, welcome to the family—His forever family, dear sister in Christ.

VIEWER GUIDE
SESSION 2

THE BEAUTY OF A WOMAN'S SEXUALITY

The _____ of God's Word:
"Be transformed by the renewing of your mind ..." (Rom. 12:2).

God is God. He has spoken. His Word stands fast.
It goes from generation to generation.

God wants to _____ His image in us.

God is a _____ God.

Everything in our temple is to say "_____" to Him.

Just as salvation is a covenant, so is your relationship
with your _____ a covenant.

_____ is a solemn binding agreement, where two become one.

If you belong to God, _____ _____ is _____ _____,
and you are to glorify God in your body.

THE GIFT YOU CAN ONLY

Give Once

At one time, a woman's virginity was a priceless treasure to be protected at all costs. The man who won her heart would win her body. He would be the first and the last to ever "know" her in this way while both lived. Their covenant relationship, confirmed by the proof of her purity, offered her security and protected them both.

Too many people today consider virginity as outdated. People are looking for love in all the wrong places, and sex is viewed as the door to love. In reality, according to the Bible, love and marriage open the door to sex.

Please hear and embrace the truth of God's Word on this important topic as you study this week. While our culture changes and each generation must be taught, God's standards never change. I'm proud of you, precious one, and I'm praying for you.

THIS WEEK, THROUGH YOUR
HOME STUDY, YOU WILL:

grow in love for and obedience
to God and His Word

(If single), *commit* to remain a virgin
until marriage to the man God provides

understand what it means to be
a pure virgin

discover how Old Testament teachings
on sexuality apply today

begin to think and act using God's Word
as a plumb line

GOD'S WORD:
THE PLUMB LINE

Have you thought much about what we studied last week, my friend, my sister—or could it be *my daughter?* In studying and writing Old Testament Precept courses that have taken us from Genesis through the historical books and on to the prophets, I've been so touched by the amazing righteous but tender heart of God for His people. It has brought me to tears. God, the Creator of the heavens and the earth, likens His relationship to His chosen people Israel to that of marriage! Fascinating, isn't it? It's a portrait God uses to give us a visual picture of our relationship with Him that we can understand—not only of what infidelity does to us but also to Him! In Ezekiel He said, "I have been hurt by their adulterous hearts which turned away from Me" (6:9).

We saw it last week: Although Israel was the wife of God, they were a people who forgot God, who played the harlot with many lovers. As God cried to them in Jeremiah, "O generation, heed the word of the LORD" (2:31), I cannot help but think of us—you and me, our daughters, our granddaughters. "Heed the word of the LORD." I think, *But as a nation we do not even know the word of God! Many of our church members probably read more of the writings of men and women than we do of God!*

This, dear one, is why I am taking the time to write this study— I want to capture your heart for the Word of God. I want you to long passionately to know every book of the Bible so that you might know your God and be equipped for every good work of life as 2 Timothy 3:16-17 says. I don't want you to be ashamed when you see Him face to face; instead, when you stand at the judgment seat of Christ as a child of God, I want you to be able to hear Him say, "Well done, my good and faithful servant."

Reason with me: You can't *heed* what you don't know, and this is where the church is statistically. Less than one-fifth of believers in the

United States of America have a biblical worldview. In other words, the Word of God is not the plumb line by which we measure the culture and make our choices. Many of us are so oblivious to the holiness, righteousness, and justice of God that we think we can call ourselves Christians, go to church, and yet live, dress, act, think, and behave like the world!

God went on to say, "Why do My people say, 'We are free to roam; We will no longer come to You'?" (Jer. 2:31). Did you notice the word *free?* Do they think because they are chosen they can get away with it? Or that God doesn't mean what He says? That He doesn't watch over His word to perform it—whether in blessing or in judgment? *Free?* No child of God is free from obedience to the Word of God—it is His Word!

Then He asked, "Can a virgin forget her ornaments, or a bride her attire? Yet My people have forgotten Me days without number. How well you prepare your way to seek love! Therefore even the wicked women you have taught your ways" (Jer. 2:32-33). In other words, God's people have so disregarded Him that they have become the teachers of the wicked! How often do you see ungodly people pointing out the sins and failures of those who profess to be children of God? They are quick to do it because in their eyes it excuses them and makes them not look so bad.

GOD'S PORTRAIT OF RELATIONSHIP
Oh, beloved, may we look at *His* portrait of the relationship of the man and the woman and learn our lesson. May we never forget that the picture comes into even tighter focus in the New Testament, where God demonstrated our relationship to Jesus Christ as the bride to the heavenly bridegroom—and the wedding day, which, by the way, is rapidly approaching.

And how does God desire to present us to His Son on that day? He expressed it through the apostle Paul in his second letter to the Corinthians, "I am jealous for you with a godly jealousy; for I betrothed you to one husband, so that to Christ I might present you as a pure virgin" (2 Cor. 11:2). It's interesting, isn't it, to watch the word *virgin* surface in respect to our relationship to our heavenly bridegroom?

The context of the above passage is false teachers and wrong teaching. Teaching that "as the serpent deceived Eve by his craftiness" would cause "your minds" to be "led astray from the simplicity and purity of devotion to Christ" (2 Cor. 11:3). You see the analogy, don't you?

Let's consider the picture God has given us in the use of the words a "pure virgin." A virgin is a virgin. But what is a pure virgin? Could it be indicating the purity connected with her virginity? Not just a woman who has never had sexual intercourse with a man, been penetrated by a man. *Pure* virgin seems to take it to another level, and you need to understand this.

"Having sex" has been grossly misinterpreted from the day a president of the United States publicly stated he had not had sex with a White House intern. A pure virgin is not a woman who simply declares herself a virgin. A pure virgin is not someone who is saying, "I've never had sex" and yet who voluntarily (without coercion or threats) has delighted in being fondled by a man and who in turn (without coercion or threats) has delighted the man with her fondling or other attempts to satisfy him apart from the actual act of intercourse.

The treasure God gave a woman is to be hidden, kept under lock and key until it is God's time to share it with another. Our focus is virginity—the gift you can give only once. Now, listen carefully, precious one. I realize someone may have forced the opening of your treasure— and God knows that and He has a word of healing for you. Or you might have foolishly given it away. I know reading all this can bring such pain that you want to throw this book across the room and walk away in bitter hopelessness. Don't do it—whatever your situation.

God is God—and because He is a God of mercy and lovingkindness and forgiveness there is hope, there is a cure. Note I said "cure." Healing is for those who know God and believe His Word. So we are going to cover it all—but obviously I can only do one thing at a time. So "hangeth thou in there with me"—I am for you, because that is the heart of our Redeemer toward you. A redeemer is someone who buys back the situation or person and brings good and value out of it!

OLD TESTAMENT EXPECTATIONS

Let's start in Deuteronomy, one of the first five books of the Bible. Collectively these five books are called the book of the Law, the Torah, or the Pentateuch. It's in this passage that you will see the value placed on a woman's virginity. The case brought up here explains what is to be done if a husband claims his wife was not a virgin when he married her.

Read Deuteronomy 22:13-21 for yourself. As you read, either color every occurrence of the word *virgin* (and *virginity*) or put a big *V* over it.
(The reason I use various colors for key repeated words that are so important to the text, is because colors are easier to distinguish than a bunch of symbols all in the same color.)

DEUTERONOMY 22:13-21

13 "If any man takes a wife and goes in to her and then turns against her,

14 and charges her with shameful deeds and publicly defames her, and says, 'I took this woman, but when I came near her, I did not find her a virgin,'

15 then the girl's father and her mother shall take and bring out the evidence of the girl's virginity to the elders of the city at the gate.

16 "The girl's father shall say to the elders, 'I gave my daughter to this man for a wife, but he turned against her;

17 and behold, he has charged her with shameful deeds, saying, 'I did not find your daughter a virgin.' But this is the evidence of my daughter's virginity.' And they shall spread the garment before the elders of the city.

18 "So the elders of that city shall take the man and chastise him,

19 and they shall fine him a hundred shekels of silver and give it to the girl's father, because he publicly defamed a virgin of Israel. And she shall remain his wife; he cannot divorce her all his days.

20 "But if this charge is true, that the girl was not found a virgin,

21 then they shall bring out the girl to the doorway of her father's house, and the men of her city shall stone her to death because she has committed an act of folly in Israel by playing the harlot in her father's house; thus you shall purge the evil from among you."

Whenever you observe the Word of God to discover what it says, remember you need to ask the **5 W's and an H:** Who, what, when, where, why and how. The who—people, God, the Devil or angels—are always the easiest to see. So begin with the easiest, the most obvious.

Who are the various people in this scenario? List them below.

Now **what** is this passage about? What is the subject—the theme or focus?

Now list everything you learn from marking the word *virgin*. Only get your answers from the text. Think about it and we will discuss it tomorrow.

As you bring this study time to an end, what's on your heart? What are your questions? Your concerns? List them somewhere and then take them all to the Lord in prayer. When you lay these things at His feet and ask for His wisdom and His understanding, it takes your relationship with God to a greater depth. You're talking with God—with your Father—about matters important to Him and to you.

DAY TWO

A TREASURE
TO PROTECT

Let's begin our time together by refreshing our minds with the truths we have seen up to this point. As we learned yesterday, a virgin is a woman who has never had sexual intercourse with a man or become one flesh with someone. And how important was this? Remember yesterday you were looking at the Word of God, the law of God, the statutes by which Israel was to live. These were God's laws, not man's.

So how important was a woman's virginity?

According to the verses in Deuteronomy, what was the proof of a woman's virginity?

Think about this. When God created woman, He made her distinctively different from the man. When you look at a baby, the major *visible* distinctive is the reproductive equipment. The doctor or the nurse looks at the baby and proclaims the child a boy or a girl on the basis of anatomy. In Psalm 139 we learn that it is God who forms us in our mother's womb.

DISTINCTIVELY DIFFERENT

When we talk about a woman's virginity, I want to make sure we have a clear understanding of the term. As women it is good for us to discuss these things together. You may not realize it, but some women are in the dark about this subject. Perhaps no one has taken the time to teach them. Or it has been done in a mixed classroom, which I don't believe is where sex should be taught. You get information, but you're too embarrassed to ask questions in front of the guys—and I respect that! So here we go!

When God created woman, she was given a vagina, where she is to receive her husband in the oneness of intercourse. From there the man's seminal fluid filled with sperm containing seeds of life travels to the uterus of the woman, where, if God so ordains, a sperm of God's choosing penetrates an egg produced by the woman and a child is wondrously created from the union of the sperm and the egg. The psalmist explained it this way, "You formed me in my mother's womb."

Across the entrance to the vagina is a hymen, a mucous membrane that partially seals the entrance into the vagina, leaving only an adequate space for the woman's menstrual discharge. It is as if God sealed a woman's virginity so that she might present it to her husband as a gift for him to unwrap on the sacred day in which they become one flesh.

This is part of the beauty of a woman's sexuality—giving a gift she can only give once in a lifetime. Is it any wonder that when God finished creating man and woman, He saw that "it was very good"?

A BIBLICAL WEDDING CEREMONY

From all that we can piece together from various Scriptures, there wasn't an exchange of vows in a marriage ceremony as we observe in our Western culture today. Rather, a covenant agreement was made that pledged a woman to a man in marriage. Although the contract could be made long before the actual marriage took place, it was a binding agreement not to be broken unless it could be proven that the woman was not a virgin. Does this bring to mind the Gospel of Matthew and what Joseph wanted to do when he found out that Mary, the mother of Jesus, was with child? His solution was to write her a bill of divorcement and put her away quietly—at least, until an angel revealed to Joseph that Mary was carrying God's Son. But let's return to the wedding ceremony.

When the time of the actual wedding came, the bride and her family would spend the day decorating the house, preparing food, getting the bride ready for her bridegroom, and dressing the bride in her bridal garments. Then when it was time and all things were made ready in the house of the bridegroom, the bridegroom would send his friends to get his bride. Torches aflame, the joyous procession lit up the black velvet of night as they went to get the bride and bring her to the bridegroom's house. All those invited to the wedding feast—the virgins with their oil lamps, the men with their torches—would turn out dressed in their wedding garments. It was a boisterous and exciting occasion, awakening the whole town as neighbors scurried to their flat roofs to catch a glimpse of the bride. As the bride neared the home of her bridegroom, all would hear the shout, "Behold the bridegroom comes" as he went out to meet his wife of the covenant.

Once inside the bridegroom's home or the tents set up on his land, the bride and the groom would slip away to the bridal tent or bridal chamber to consummate their pledge. It was said the bridegroom was "to go into his bride." Over the bridal bed would be a canopy, a *chuppah*, while under the bride would be her bridal garment or cloth. The blood on the garment or cloth would attest to her virginity, as her husband sealed the covenant of blood "by passing through pieces of her flesh."

The two were now one. The marriage was now consummated. The bridal garment, stained with the blood of the covenant, would be wrapped up and put away. It was proof of her virginity, the beauty of her sexuality. Now do you have a better understanding of why God hates divorce and adultery?

Read Matthew 19:3-9. As you do, mark:
  - Every reference to *divorce*, including "let no man separate," in a distinctive color or with a big **D**.
  - Adultery with a big **A**.

MATTHEW 19:3-9

³ Some Pharisees came to Jesus, testing Him and asking, "Is it lawful for a man to divorce his wife for any reason at all?"

⁴ And He answered and said, "Have you not read that He who created them from the beginning MADE THEM MALE AND FEMALE,

⁵ and said, 'FOR THIS REASON A MAN SHALL LEAVE HIS FATHER AND MOTHER AND BE JOINED TO HIS WIFE, AND THE TWO SHALL BECOME ONE FLESH'?

⁶ So they are no longer two, but one flesh. What therefore God has joined together, let no man separate."

⁷ They said to Him, "Why then did Moses command to GIVE HER A CERTIFICATE OF DIVORCE AND SEND HER AWAY?"

⁸ He said to them, "Because of your hardness of heart Moses permitted you to divorce your wives; but from the beginning it has not been this way.

⁹ "And I say to you, whoever divorces his wife, except for immorality, and marries another woman commits adultery."

List what you learned from marking references to *divorce*.

Look at where you marked *adultery.* In light of what you learned about virginity and purity, why would marrying another person constitute adultery?

A SERIOUS MATTER TO GOD

Did you notice the Scriptures Jesus quoted from Genesis as He answered the Pharisees in Matthew 19? First, marriage is to be between a man and a woman; God made them male and female. Second, the two become one flesh. Intercourse with another person violates the picture of one flesh. Therefore, to leave your mate except because of his or her sexual immorality, which violates your oneness, is considered adultery in the eyes of God. Our God-given sexuality is a serious matter with God.

Well, dear one, as you think about all of this, do you understand that there was a time when a woman's virginity was a priceless treasure to be protected at all costs? The man who would win her heart would win her body. He would be the first and the last to ever know her while both lived—and *there* was her security and their protection from little foxes that would rob the vine of its pure and delightful fruit, as Song of Solomon 2:15 says.

Oh, precious one, if you are hurting because you were not a virgin when you married or because you were robbed of your virginity by someone who sexually abused you, raped you, or took advantage of you, talk to God about it. Then we'll talk about it. Pour out your heart to God; He tells us He is near to the brokenhearted.

And if you are still a virgin—thank God, and write out your resolve. Make a commitment to God to walk in obedience to His Word and honor the beauty of your sexuality.

WHEN GOD'S HEART IS GRIEVED

Unfortunately, many in our society today take virginity lightly. It's something scoffed at, almost a reproach, because you haven't gotten with it, or no one has found you desirable. Virginity is outdated because morality is almost extinct. Sex outside of marriage carries no shame or guilt.

How very sad. How grievous to the heart of God such attitudes must be since chastity before marriage was obviously God's plan since before creation.

I want us to look at two more passages from the Torah, God's law, that reveal the importance of a woman's virginity.

Let's return to Deuteronomy 22 and study verses 22-29. As you observe the text:
- **Color-code every reference to the woman (girl), including pronouns.** If you don't know what color to use—be traditional, go for pink!
- **Mark the references to *virgin* as you did earlier.** Remember, I suggested a big *V*.
- **Mark all references to death and dying.** I draw a black tombstone like this: ⌂.
- **Remember when you see the word *engaged*, it means "betrothed"; a covenant has been made.**

DEUTERONOMY 22:22-29

²² "If a man is found lying with a married woman, then both of them shall die, the man who lay with the woman, and the woman; thus you shall purge the evil from Israel.
²³ "If there is a girl who is a virgin engaged to a man, and another man finds her in the city and lies with her,

²⁴ then you shall bring them both out to the gate of that city and you shall stone them to death; the girl, because she did not cry out in the city, and the man, because he has violated his neighbor's wife. Thus you shall purge the evil from among you.

²⁵ "But if in the field the man finds the girl who is engaged, and the man forces her and lies with her, then only the man who lies with her shall die.

²⁶ "But you shall do nothing to the girl; there is no sin in the girl worthy of death, for just as a man rises against his neighbor and murders him, so is this case.

²⁷ "When he found her in the field, the engaged girl cried out, but there was no one to save her.

²⁸ "If a man finds a girl who is a virgin, who is not engaged, and seizes her and lies with her and they are discovered,

²⁹ "then the man who lay with her shall give to the girl's father fifty shekels of silver, and she shall become his wife because he has violated her; he cannot divorce her all his days."

As you read these laws, you find they cover several scenarios. Let's look at them one by one. As you do, look at the words that you marked and write down what the situation is with the woman, what is to be done, and why.

DEUTERONOMY 22:22

DEUTERONOMY 22:23-24

DEUTERONOMY 22:25-27

DEUTERONOMY 22:28-29

Before you explain what happens in these verses, read
the text again and mark, as you did before, any reference
to divorce using a big black *D*.

Now, beloved, as you reflected on these verses, who
and what were being protected?

What does this tell you about God's heart in respect
to the beauty of a woman's sexuality?

Now, let's take a quick look at Exodus 22:16-17.
Mark every reference to a virgin.

EXODUS 22:16-17
16 "If a man seduces a virgin who is not engaged, and lies with
   her, he must pay a dowry for her to be his wife.
17 "If her father absolutely refuses to give her to him, he shall
   pay money equal to the dowry for virgins.

Based on what you have read, is a woman always to marry the man who takes away her virginity?

Is the man responsible to the woman in any way if she refuses to marry him? Explain your answer.

What does this show you about the value God places on a woman's virginity?

How does this make you feel?

I know as you've studied for the past three days that you may be among those who wish that they had waited until marriage. Your heart may be filled with regret because you foolishly, unthinkingly, gave away the one gift that can only be given once. Maybe you gave it to someone you didn't even know, someone you didn't care about. Perhaps you were raped or sexually abused.

Maybe you know someone who wishes she had waited. You have an awesome opportunity to minister and support others through what you are learning. The following letter offers a dramatic example.

I am lucky to have a loving, moral family whose members are our top priorities. My parents are now in their 34th year of marriage and have remained faithful and true to each other through it all … a rarity today.

Unfortunately for me, however, those high moral standards meant I felt I was alone when it came to dealing with life issues. My parents thought good moral people didn't talk or think about sexuality and sexual matters. I lived a good life because I never had to confront temptations. I figured that people who run around with a wild crowd and party all the time are the only ones who have to deal with temptation. …

Being born with limited sight and being sheltered, I was anything but popular and included at school and at college. Because I'm legally blind, I can't drive, so I withdrew into my family and didn't seem to mature. While my peers and classmates learned the ropes of life with friends, began to date, and became seriously involved and even married their sweethearts, I went on living as a little girl in the comfort of the family.

Then I began to rebel. I couldn't take all the teasing for being immature and not knowing how to have fun. I tried so hard to be included, but when others saw how naïve I was, they turned elsewhere, leaving me all alone. I literally had no social life. I went home from college every weekend and buried myself in my studies and writing projects—novelettes I never completed.

Then came my senior year of college. I saw my required internship at a local radio station as my first shot at becoming normal by becoming involved with an older man (we'll call him Don). This was where my real rebellion against my parents began. I was almost 21 and had never dated anyone, but when I met Don, I decided that if he were single, he would be the man for me. He was 34, divorced, and had a 13-year-old son.

I did all I could to pursue him, including things that went totally against our family values, such as how I dressed. Suddenly my life became one massive deception. With my family I conveniently avoided the subject of Don. In many ways I knew he wasn't my type. Much I learned about him really bothered me, but I was finally free—and I didn't care!

Finally, my plan worked and he asked me out. My parents were supportive and let me go. It was really fun—miniature golf, hours of just talking at his apartment, and my first kiss. As we dated, we started experimenting more sexually. On our third date Don showed me my first X-rated movie after an afternoon at the mall and dinner at a restaurant.

Eventually, I hesitatingly accepted Don's insistence that all normal girls do it and love it. It was all so gross, so perverted that I ended up in psychological counseling. With the help of my therapist I tried to return to a decent life, but the nightmares kept haunting me.

When I eventually got involved at a local Christian television station, it was like beginning anew, although the scars remained. Then I was saved, but I was confused as I sought out the truth. When I found your teaching ministry on television, all of a sudden I knew. You taught me much in the area of my sexuality that I had never really dealt with, and the lingering brokenness finally left.

I feel like a virgin again.

Because it is a gift we only give one time, once it is given or taken, that is it. All the sorrow, all the tears, all the "if only's" will never bring it back. But you can, dear one, like my friend, "feel like a virgin again." God can restore a purity to your life, as He cleanses you with the water of His Word that He might present you to Himself as a chaste virgin, a bride without blemish, without spot or wrinkle (Eph. 5:25-26).

This is the beauty of belonging to God, to a Sovereign God who is the Redeemer—to One who is able to make the following promise. (There is also a warning, but I want us to focus on the promise!)

Before we read this promise, though, let me give you the definition of the following terms. It will come in handy as we continue our study.

- The word *fornicators* (Greek: *pornos*) in this passage carries the idea of selling. Therefore this is the selling of oneself for sexual purposes. "A whoremonger or male prostitute. In the NT a fornicator. The Greeks considered one who prostituted himself for gain as a *pórnos*."[2]
- Adulterers (Greek: *moichos*): a person who participates in unlawful intercourse
- Effeminate (Greek: *malakós*): "Soft to the touch, spoken of clothing made of soft materials, fine texture. Figuratively it means effeminate or a person who allows himself to be sexually abused contrary to nature."[3]
- Homosexuals (*arsenokoítës*) from *ársën* a male, and *koítë*, a bed. A man who lies in bed with another male, a homosexual.[4]

Now, on to the promise. As you read the following Scripture, circle every reference to *sexual sin* and color-code every occurrence of the word *you*.

I CORINTHIANS 6:9-11

9 Or do you not know that the unrighteous will not inherit the kingdom of God? Do not be deceived; neither fornicators, nor idolaters, nor adulterers, nor effeminate, nor homosexuals,

10 nor thieves, nor the covetous, nor drunkards, nor revilers, nor swindlers, will inherit the kingdom of God.

11 Such were some of you; but you were washed, but you were sanctified, but you were justified in the name of the Lord Jesus Christ and in the Spirit of our God.

I love watching before-and-afters, don't you, beloved? I think it must be a woman thing!

What before-and-after do you see when you look at all the *you's* **you marked?**

What does that tell you about God?

Our God is awesome, isn't He? Now, beloved, bring your study to a close by asking God what He wants you to do with what you are learning. Ask Him to lead you to others to whom you can minister with these truths. Sometimes it helps to write down the thoughts He brings to mind.

LIVING IN LIGHT OF
GOD'S WORD

A great many of America's founding fathers had a holy reverence of the Word of God. Primers that taught children to read often included the Ten Commandments. It was the Ten Commandments and the Word of God that helped shaped the character of the United States. Immorality was not acceptable behavior. The sins listed in I Corinthians 6:9-10, including the sexual misbehaviors you marked, were punishable by law because such behavior destroys a nation.

> **Let's look at the Ten Commandments for a moment to better understand how special our sexuality is and how society is to guard it. Read them aloud carefully and then:**
> - Number the Commandments.
> - Color every reference to anything that has to do with what God says is sexually immoral.

When you come to the final Commandment, you will come across the word *covet*. Since covet is not a frequently used word, let me give you a definition. In the Hebrew, covet is *hamad* and it means, "to lust, desire," for example, strongly desire another's possessions.[5]

EXODUS 20:1-17
1 Then God spoke all these words, saying,
2 "I am the LORD your God, who brought you out of the land of Egypt, out of the house of slavery.
3 "You shall have no other gods before Me.
4 "You shall not make for yourself an idol, or any likeness of what is in heaven above or on the earth beneath or in the water under the earth.

⁵ "You shall not worship them or serve them; for I, the LORD your God, am a jealous God, visiting the iniquity of the fathers on the children, on the third and the fourth generations of those who hate Me,

⁶ "but showing lovingkindness to thousands, to those who love Me and keep My commandments.

⁷ "You shall not take the name of the LORD your God in vain, for the LORD will not leave him unpunished who takes His name in vain.

⁸ "Remember the sabbath day, to keep it holy.

⁹ "Six days you shall labor and do all your work,

¹⁰ "but the seventh day is a sabbath of the LORD your God; in it you shall not do any work, you or your son or your daughter, your male or your female servant or your cattle or your sojourner who stays with you.

¹¹ "For in six days the LORD made the heavens and the earth, the sea and all that is in them, and rested on the seventh day; therefore the LORD blessed the sabbath day and made it holy.

¹² "Honor your father and your mother, that your days may be prolonged in the land which the LORD your God gives you.

¹³ "You shall not murder.

¹⁴ "You shall not commit adultery.

¹⁵ "You shall not steal.

¹⁶ "You shall not bear false witness against your neighbor.

¹⁷ "You shall not covet your neighbor's house; you shall not covet your neighbor's wife or his male servant or his female servant or his ox or his donkey or anything that belongs to your neighbor."

Which of the Ten Commandments has to do with our sexuality?

What do they tell you about the value God places
on our sexuality?

How do these Commandments fit into the culture
of today—and why?

Do you think they fit differently into our culture because
our culture is different? Because we are not under
a theocracy today but a democratic republic, is there
any area for compromise? Why or why not?

Leviticus gives us greater details of the Law, as do the chapters that
follow the listing of the Ten Commandments.

Now, before I ask more questions, let's look at
Leviticus 20:7-10. As you read these verses, mark:
- Every occurrence of the pronoun *you.*
- The references to *adultery* as you have done previously.
- Mark the references to *death.* Remember the black tombstone!
- The word *sanctifies* means "to set apart, to consecrate."
  The words *holy, sanctify,* and *consecrate* all have the same basic
  meaning. Put a ⛅ around these words.

LEVITICUS 20:7-10

7 "You shall consecrate yourselves therefore and be holy, for I am the LORD your God.

8 "You shall keep My statutes and practice them; I am the LORD who sanctifies you.

9 If there is anyone who curses his father or his mother, he shall surely be put to death; he has cursed his father or his mother, his bloodguiltiness is upon him.

10 "If there is a man who commits adultery with another man's wife, one who commits adultery with his friend's wife, the adulterer and the adulteress shall surely be put to death."

What do you learn from marking the occurrences of *you?* List your insights below.

If you are a child of God, there is a higher law: God's. How do you measure up to the *you's* you marked?

What did you learn from marking the references to adultery and death?

What insight does this passage give you into God, His commands, and our sexuality?

Because we are not the nation of Israel and do not live under a theocracy as they once did, we are not going to put people to death when they break God's commands even though God said they are to die.

However, does this excuse us, as children of God, from keeping His commands? _____ Why?

As we bring today to a close, let me share a letter I received from a young man after speaking at a college Christmas conference for Campus Crusade for Christ. It so touched my heart.

> I was blown away when I heard you speak. I did not realize the extent of your powerful testimony that dealt with sexual immorality. It soon became clear that this issue is close to your heart (God's Word no less), as your words began to pierce my heart like arrows.
>
> You see, at the time my girlfriend and I were in a terrible habit of overstepping our boundaries. Early on in our relationship we set boundaries that demonstrated our desire to uphold God's best for our relationship. These boundaries lasted for roughly 12 months. As our relationship approached one year in length, we began to struggle much more with our flesh.
>
> After attending the conference in Knoxville, it soon became very clear that the Lord was speaking to my heart. As the conviction took its course, I began to realize that sexual immorality (Gal. 5:19) didn't mean only

not having intercourse (or coming close to the action thereof); instead, it was compromising God's desire for our bodies to be treated as temples of worship unto Him (Rom. 12:1-2).

As I brought back to our relationship my convictions from the conference and the tapes of your talk, it became clear to us both that we needed to seek God's redemption and to rely on His strength to obtain purity in our relationship.

In the past eight months we have come to have purity and peace like never before. We have grown in our love and in following Christ as well as in our respect for one another. We are now engaged and plan in eight months to share in the sacrament of marriage and unite as one flesh. We have promised one another as a sign of our desire for purity to avoid any and all forms of kissing and physical contact (with the exception of holding hands) until the proper time and to avoid the opportunity for temptation.

What an awesome wedding night this couple will have! No guilt. No regrets. Instead, there will be a beauty, a purity, a special quality about it, a sweet sense of God's blessing it wouldn't have had if they had not heard and obeyed God's Word.

How odd this couple is in a society like ours! The statistics at the turn of the second millennium showed that those who considered themselves Christians were as immoral as those who didn't even claim to know God. Can you imagine how obeying just this one passage of Scripture would change the church and impact society? The world would no longer have an excuse to cover their immorality. They would see that purity until marriage is possible and rewarding.

Do you realize that those who live together before they get married have a higher divorce rate than those who wait until marriage? Could it be that we might be on to something about a marriage that lasts if we will just listen to God?

So is there any such thing as "safe sex"? Hint: Look back at I Thessalonians 4.

How would you answer this question if you were to listen to what God has to say about sex?

Finally, because I care about you, I have to ask, How are you going to live in the light of what God has to say on the subject?

DAY FIVE

SO WHAT ABOUT THE MAN?

In the light of all we've studied this week, let me ask you a question. Is it as people have thought for generations—that the woman is to remain a virgin until marriage but not the man? Maybe you've heard similar words: *After all, he is a man! And men, well, because they are men, they have to have sex! God knows how strong that male sex drive is, how easily it is triggered by what a man sees, hears, and thinks. God ought to know: He's the One who made man like he is, with sex on the brain. No, God doesn't expect a man to wait!*

Of course, a man is usually the one offering this rationale. He's a man. He understands the sex drive and how he can be so easily turned on simply by what he sees! He faces battles night and day once those hormones kick in.

But what did God say? That is what we need to know, isn't it? Does God not expect a man to be a virgin since He only deals with the woman's virginity in the passage we studied in Deuteronomy? The word *virgin* is never used for a man. Is God letting us know that a man's virginity doesn't count with God, that God doesn't expect that of him?

Let's look at two passages of Scripture and see what you think after you read them.

First, let's look at Proverbs 5:15-23. Proverbs 5:1 begins with, "My son, give attention to my wisdom." As you read the verses that follow this admonition, mark or color every reference to the son, which of course will include all pronouns such as "you" or "your." Begin with verse 15.

PROVERBS 5:15-23

15 Drink water from your own cistern
   And fresh water from your own well.
16 Should your springs be dispersed abroad,
   Streams of water in the streets?
17 Let them be yours alone
   And not for strangers with you.
18 Let your fountain be blessed,
   And rejoice in the wife of your youth.
19 As a loving hind and a graceful doe,
   Let her breasts satisfy you at all times;
   Be exhilarated always with her love.
20 For why should you, my son, be exhilarated with an adulteress
   And embrace the bosom of a foreigner?
21 For the ways of a man are before the eyes of the LORD,
   And He watches all his paths.
22 His own iniquities will capture the wicked,
   And he will be held with the cords of his sin.
23 He will die for lack of instruction,
   And in the greatness of his folly he will go astray.

Read this passage again. In the light of its context, what
do you think the father meant when he used the imagery
of water, cistern, and then the term "your springs"?

What words in this passage tell you where a man is to get
his sexual satisfaction?

SATISFIED AT HOME

God used the words in Proverbs 5 to say that a man's sexual desires are to
be satisfied at home. The breasts of his wife are to be his satisfaction, not
the breasts of some stranger, some prostitute, or some immoral woman.
He is to drink water from his own well, his own wife, when he thirsts for
sexual satisfaction. His springs—his sperm—are not to be dispersed all
over town, up and down the streets, given to one woman after another!
His life, his DNA, and his genes are in his sperm.

The man's sperm determines the sexuality of a child. He makes sons
and daughters! It's sacred. He's in partnership with the Creator of all
life, the One who formed him—us—in our mother's womb. The One
who numbers our days even before we are born! A man's sperm is to be
his, raised in his family, bearing his name, inheriting his inheritance. A
man's sperm is a man's future. There is only one place a man's seed is to
be sown—with the wife of his youth.

A man is to know and to raise his children. Don't we want to know
who our father is? Do you remember the word people would hurl at
children born out of wedlock—*Bastard!* Horrible, isn't it? Why would
a man do this to a child just to satisfy his own desires? What kind of a
man is this?

Oh dear one, if you are a mother, instruct your daughter in matters
like this. Or if you are single or considering marriage, think these things

through. What do you want in a husband? Write it down. Store it in a safe place or in a file on your computer. The best-looking, most popular guys do not always make the best husbands! Watch how a man treats other women. Consider his values, his family, and how he was raised. Sometimes as women we have what I call a lame puppy-type of compassion; we see a wounded, hurting, troubled young man and we think that we can fix him, that we can be his savior. You don't want a man you have to fix to be your husband! Unfortunately, because we as a society have lost the fear of God, the presence of the mother in the home, and the devotion of the father to his family, increasingly more men need a lot of fixing. Just remember you are not the Savior!

Now, let's look at 1 Corinthians 7. The letters of 1 and 2 Corinthians were written to a church that was birthed through the apostle Paul, a church that lived in a city steeped in immorality. You just saw that when you looked at the verses from 1 Corinthians 6:9-11. Many of these people were such fornicators and adulterers, indulging in all sorts of sexual sin, that a term was coined in their name: to *corinthianize*, which meant to be involved in sexual debauchery.

In 1 Corinthians 7 Paul addressed some questions the church had raised to him. The time is the first century A.D. This church was comprised of people who had "corinthianized" in the past and were now being Christianized. No wonder they had questions!

As Paul answered these questions, I think he also provided God's answer about men remaining virgins, not having sex until marriage, or staying pure if they don't get married. Let's look at four verses out of this chapter.

As you read them, color-code or mark the following in a way that enables you to tell one from another. Underline anything that relates to marriage.
- *man*
- *immoralities*
- *self-control*

I CORINTHIANS 7:1-2,8-9

¹ Now concerning the things about which you wrote, it is
good for a man not to touch a woman.

² But because of immoralities, each man is to have his own
wife, and each woman is to have her own husband.

⋯⋯⋯⋯⋯⋯⋯⋯⋯⋯⋯⋯⋯⋯⋯⋯⋯⋯⋯⋯⋯⋯⋯

⁸ But I say to the unmarried and to widows that it is good
for them if they remain even as I. *[Paul was not married
when he wrote this.]*

⁹ But if they do not have self-control, let them marry;
for it is better to marry than to burn with passion.

Let me give you a side note before we go on. The word *touch* in verse I
means to take a hold of a woman in a sexual manner. In classical Greek
the word meant *to light a fire.*

What did you learn from marking the references to *man?*
List your insights.

What did you learn from marking *immoralities?* What
prevents immoralities? Look at the context; it will tell you.

How does self-control fit into this? To what was Paul
referring? What's the answer to a lack of self-control?

According to these verses, what is the solution to taking
care of one's sex drive?

MARRIAGE IS GOD'S ANSWER

If a man is burning with sexual desire, he is to get married. It is as simple as that! You have seen it in God's Word for yourself. You have your answer: There is to be no sex outside of marriage for the male as well as the female. Marriage is God's provision for satisfying our sex drive, and sex is to be only within the confines of marriage. Regardless of what society says or portrays, God says that a man, just like a woman, is to remain a virgin until marriage.

Jan Silvious, a dear friend of mine, is a wonderful author and a great speaker. Years ago she and I went to Daytona Beach to an ocean home someone had made available to me. I was going to write a new Precept course that the Lord had placed on my heart: *A Marriage Without Regrets.* Jan would assist, reading and doing the study and giving me feedback. We enjoyed wonderful days of studying, writing, and talking it all through during long walks on the beach. The only bad thing was our timing. It was spring break. A swarm of students out to enjoy themselves to the fullest soon covered the beaches.

As we walked the beach one afternoon, I looked from the ocean back to the houses. The shouts and cajoling of a group of young men diving off the roof of the house into the pool caught my attention. "They're crazy. They could break their necks," I said to Jan, remembering my friend who was paralyzed when he dived into a pool at camp.

"That's boys for you." Jan's response brought the conversation to a close. We both had sons, and I knew exactly what she meant.

The next day, when it was time again for our afternoon walk, I wondered if the guys were still jumping off the roof into the pool. Instead of boys on the roof, a huge sheet proclaimed with enormous lettering: "GET LAID HERE!" I was outraged. Not only were college and high school kids on the beach but also families with their little children! They shouldn't have to see that, and parents should neither have to explain it nor dodge the question.

"Someone should talk to them. That sheet has to come down." I walked about five feet farther and it was as if God said, "Kay, you talk to them."

I stopped in the sand, looked at Jan, and said, "I've got to go talk with them. Someone has to tell them, and I think God wants me to."

Jan said she'd wait and pray.

We were both in our bathing suits, obviously not college girls but certainly not over the hill either! As I walked past the sand dunes with the sea oats waving in the gentle breeze, I noticed a rush for the house. Two young men saw me coming and ran for cover. Was it a guilty conscience, or did they think I was answering their ad? Who knows? At the time, I didn't even stop to think about it. I watched as they peeped from behind the curtains like little kids.

I continued walking toward the door while I beckoned them with my finger to come out of the house. The door opened, and we stood face to face. It was an interesting conversation to say the least. I told them how I felt about the bed sheet, its message, and why. They stammered, stuttered, and sputtered, trying to say they didn't mean anything by it. What was wrong with it anyway? It was just a joke.

Then I said, "Let me ask you a question. Would you want someone to lay your sister? And what about your mother? Would you want someone laying your mother? And when you get married and have a daughter, do you want some young guy like yourself to lay your daughter?"

Of course with every question there was a shake of the head accompanied by a barely audible "No."

"Then, guys, why are you offering to lay a girl? Every girl is someone's daughter, many are someone's sister, and in all probability most will be someone's mother someday."

That is you, dear heart! A woman! A daughter! As a parent, would you want your daughter to behave as you behave? Would you want your mother to live as you are living?

As we bring our week of study to a close, remember that an immediate fulfillment of passion can birth painful memories and regrets. Don't sacrifice the beauty and purity of sex on the altar of passionate lust. Honor your Creator, your God, your Heavenly Father ... and guard the gift you can only give once.

Viewer Guide
Session 3

THE GIFT YOU CAN ONLY GIVE ONCE

God has said that sex outside of marriage is _____.

Marriage is _____ _____ for all time.

I KINGS II

Verse 1: "King Solomon loved many foreign women."

Verse 2: "Solomon held fast to these in love."

Verse 6: "Solomon … did not follow the LORD _____."

Just because you are married doesn't mean you won't be

_____.

We've got to _____ the truth. We've got to _____ it.

We've got to reset the _____.

MAN: PREDATOR OR *Protector?*

When God created man, did He intend for man to be a predator or a protector of women? This is a question you need to be able to answer biblically, and our study this week will help you do so.

Unfortunately, there are too many examples today of the man who is a predator, the man who takes advantage of women, the man who disregards or holds other people in very low esteem. Our answers must come from God, not society. And He speaks clearly on this subject in His Word.

Beloved, our study this week reinforces that you are created according to God's plan—and man's role is part of that plan. Give your best prayers and time to your home study this week. It can transform your relationship with your husband and sons and mark the beginning of healing where needed.

THIS WEEK, THROUGH YOUR
HOME STUDY, YOU WILL:

grow in love for and obedience
to God by studying His Word

identify ways the beauty of
sexuality has been distorted

compare and contrast man as predator
with God's plan for him as protector

consider personal actions in which
you can be salt and light in the world

affirm ways your husband lives as
a protector, following Christ's example

DAY ONE

When God's Plan Is
DISTORTED

In a 2007 *Christianity Today* article, Dawn Herzog Jewell wrote, "When Moon was 12 weeks old, her birth mother sold her to a local Burmese woman, who raised her like a slave. When Moon (not her real name) ... turned 13, the woman sold Moon's virginity to a Western business-man in Thailand. But she fought her way free. A few months later, she wasn't so lucky. Her second mother blocked the hotel room door after an Indian man paid 30,000 baht ($800) and then beat Moon with a belt until she submitted to sex. She had to be carried home. For 10 days, Moon couldn't walk."

Moon went from a hotel room to a brothel where she would be raped over 100 times not only by men visiting Thailand for the recre-ation of sex—but also by those on the local police force![1]

Sex trafficking of women and children is big business. According to UNICEF, an estimated one million children enter the multibillion-dollar industry of sexual exploitation annually. Did that register, my sister? **Multibillion!** And many of those children are far younger than Moon.

The business of child sex tours draws about 25 percent of its customers from the United States of America where lecherous perverts from all walks of life sacrifice the bodies of little girls created in the image of God on the hedonistic altar of their abominable lust.[2]

When God created man, did He create him to be a predator or a protector of women? This is a question you need to be able to answer biblically and to take to the women God brings into your sphere of influence so that truth ceases to stumble in the streets. I would say the greater majority of women in the world are being destroyed to one degree or another by the distorted lie of the father of lies, the serpent of old—the one who walked into the garden of Eden and slithered out after convincing woman that God didn't really mean what He said and that He was really withholding good from her. After all, with one bite of the fruit of the tree of the knowledge of good and evil, she could be like God and know good and evil for herself (Gen. 3:1-5). Consequently, women in general have experienced more evil than good. Some of them are convinced that they are unclean, undeserving, and probably brought much of their pain upon themselves because in reality they deserve it—being only a woman! What a destructive lie!

In May 2007 Charmaine Hedding from Israel and I chaired a Congress on Empowering Women Through Judeo Christian Values. We held it in Jerusalem under the auspices of the Women's Council of the Knesset Christian Allies Caucus. Statistics that I pulled from reliable Internet sources on the abuse of women said:

- Each year an estimated 113-200 million women (including little girls) are missing demographically.
- Between 1.5 and 3 million women and girls have lost their lives in the past year as a result of violence and neglect.
- Approximately 6,000 girls undergo genital mutilation daily—even in the United States!

Did God intend any of this for women, or has the beauty of sexuality been distorted? The theme for our congress in Israel was "I Am My Sister's Keeper." And we are, dear ones. Because we are our sister's keeper, we need to know for ourselves all that the Word of God says about our womanhood so we can share the truth with others and the truth can set them free. Mark and Christa Crawford did this with Moon, who, after she came to know Jesus Christ, said, "I have realized that I have value and worth. And now that I know God, I can always pray for his help whenever I have a problem."[3]

I want to set the stage for our subject by returning to Genesis 2. God sets the stage for a man's relationship to the woman He created for him.

Read aloud Genesis 2:21-25, printed for you on page 72.

GENESIS 2:21-25

[21] So the LORD God caused a deep sleep to fall upon the man,
and he slept; then He took one of his ribs and closed up
the flesh at that place.

[22] The LORD God fashioned into a woman the rib which He
had taken from the man, and brought her to the man.

[23] The man said,

"This is now bone of my bones,

And flesh of my flesh;

She shall be called Woman,

Because she was taken out of Man."

[24] For this reason a man shall leave his father and his mother,
and be joined to his wife; and they shall become one flesh.

[25] And the man and his wife were both naked and were not
ashamed.

**Read these verses again and mark every reference to the
LORD God, including pronouns. When you finish, list below
what you learn from marking these references.**

**Read through the text again and mark every reference to
the *man* in one way, to the *woman* in another, and to sin
in another way. Include pronouns in your marking.**

Look at the places where you marked the *man*. What was the man's response to this woman God gave him? List your insights. Put down every last detail—don't add to the text, just don't miss it!

From what you've read, would you see man as simply being neutral toward a woman with no interest, no responsibility? A likely predator? By *predator* I mean someone who is going to prey on others, take advantage of them, use others for his or her pleasure or desire even at the other's expense. Or would you go so far as to say man is a protector? (Think now; this is before Genesis 3 when sin entered into the world.)

Complete this sentence:
I see man as _____ in this passage because

Finally, precious lady, from what you observe from marking
woman, **how do you think the woman saw herself in respect**
to the man, and why?

An estimated one of every three women in the United States has been abused by a man. As I sit propped up in bed writing this and healing from a broken ankle, I realize you could be a woman who has been misused or abused by a man. If that is the case, please hold three truths in your hurting heart.

First, beloved, what has been done to you makes God angry. Unless that person repents, God will deal with him in the severest way possible. *Second,* I want you to know you can be healed.[4] *Third,* God is the Redeemer. If you are His child through believing in Jesus Christ and receiving God's forgiveness of your sins, He will bring good out of your sorrows. God promises that and He stands by His Word!

Let's spend some time now talking to God and listening to His answers. Whatever your circumstances, dear sister, would you take time to pray for our sisters in the flesh by virtue of being born a woman and for our sisters in the Spirit by virtue of being born again into God's forever family? Would you ask God in these dark days to show us how to bring to light the sanctity of a woman's sexuality and His impending judgment on all who violate women?

Would you ask God to return a fear of Him to this world? Would you tell God that you want to get this message out to your peers, daughters, and your daughter's friends so there is a return to purity? Such a movement for morality happened in England in the days of William Wilberforce. It could happen again if every true child of God made being God's salt and light a priority (Matt. 5:13-16) and if our ambition is to be pleasing to Him (2 Cor. 5:9).

DAY TWO

MAN AS
STEWARD

I didn't want to say too much about Genesis 2:22-25 yesterday until we looked at a corresponding passage in Ephesians 5:25-33. If you have any question at all about the role of a man in respect to woman, today certainly ought to settle it. So often when someone teaches or preaches about marriage from Ephesians 5:22-33, the emphasis is on a wife's submission to her husband. It is clearly taught in this passage and yet seldom in the context of the whole. Understood in the context of the whole, it is so much easier to understand and receive.

However, since marriage is not the subject at hand but rather the role of a man in respect to woman as protector or predator, this is where our focus will be. I didn't want you to think I was avoiding Ephesians 5:22 and the command of God to women. (Smile, dear one!) Your assignment today is to look at the role of the husband in respect to his wife.

Read aloud Ephesians 5:25-33 and mark in a distinctive way or color the references, including pronouns, to the husband. Mark the references to the wife in another way. Underline, box, or circle every "just as," "as," and "even as."

EPHESIANS 5:25-33

25 Husbands, love your wives, just as Christ also loved the church and gave Himself up for her,

26 so that He might sanctify her, having cleansed her by the washing of water with the word,

27 that He might present to Himself the church in all her glory, having no spot or wrinkle or any such thing; but that she would be holy and blameless.

28 So husbands ought also to love their own wives as their own bodies. He who loves his own wife loves himself;

29 for no one ever hated his own flesh, but nourishes and cherishes it, just as Christ also does the church,

30 because we are members of His body.

31 FOR THIS REASON A MAN SHALL LEAVE HIS FATHER AND MOTHER AND SHALL BE JOINED TO HIS WIFE, AND THE TWO SHALL BECOME ONE FLESH.

32 This mystery is great; but I am speaking with reference to Christ and the church.

33 Nevertheless, each individual among you also is to love his own wife even as himself, and the wife must see to it that she respects her husband.

List below everything you observe from marking the references to the *husband*.

I wish I could see your face right now! How I would love to be there with you in your discussion class. It's awesome, isn't it, to see what God says about the role of a man!

But before I go any further, go back to page 72 and read again what you observed in Genesis 2. Do you see any parallels between the two passages? Write them down here.

Let's reason together. Woman is a gift to man, a gift from God. Consequently, she should be treated accordingly. How is that "accordingly" described in Ephesians 5?

"ACCORDINGLY" CHARACTERISTICS

Man is to be a steward of God's gift! He is responsible for his wife's development and well-being. Jesus Christ is his example. A husband is to love, nourish, and cherish his wife. He is not to abuse her verbally or physically or to demean her. To nourish means to rear, to feed, to bring to maturity. A husband is responsible for the growth and development of his wife. She is to be presented to Christ holy and blameless, not tainted or desecrated, but blameless. (And dear, if you are single, remember you have a heavenly bridegroom. This is His job—and He will do it, if you'll submit!)

To cherish means to heat, make warm. It carries the idea of tender love and affection. As I write this I think of our own Doris (Dorie) Van Stone, the subject of Erwin Lutzer's book, *Dorie: The Girl Nobody Loved*.[5] Although Dorie was sexually abused from her childhood and years in an orphanage, that part of her story comes later in the book *No Place To Cry*.[6] I think I was one of the first to hear of her sexual abuse—which brought with it great shame—and the fear of rejection once it was known.

God has given me the privilege of sharing much with this dear woman who made Precept Ministries International her home base for years. I know my Dorie even as I had the privilege of knowing her husband Lloyd. They lived with Jack and me close to a month during one of our summer inductive study programs. Lloyd died one day while jogging. It was after his death that Dorie shared Lloyd's patience with her when she couldn't give herself to him sexually for a period of time after they were married. It was his patience with her, his tender love and affection, that brought her to the moment when they became one flesh in fullness of its meaning. This is cherishing. This is being the protector.

FOLLOWING CHRIST'S EXAMPLE

The protector loves his wife as he loves his own flesh . . . as himself.

The protector follows Christ's example and lays down his life for his wife. This is man as God designed him to be—designed in His image.

If you have a son, think of the responsibility you and your husband have to model this relationship before his eyes. And if you have no husband at home, then you must teach this role to him by training him to treat you properly as a woman as well as his mother.

And if you are single and have nephews, it is the same for you, dear one. And you ought to model purity for him so he'll want to marry a virtuous woman just like his aunt!

As a wife I encourage you to encourage your husband, not by using this passage in Ephesians as a hammer, but as a means of illustrating your gratitude for his Christlike behavior when he comes close to loving you in this way.

I wonder, did you notice in verse 33 what the woman is to do? She is not only to submit—to arrange herself under her husband's God-ordained authority—but she is also to reverence her husband. A man has two inherent fears (remember he was designed by God): First, that of being ruled over by a woman, and second, that of being found inadequate. Men have an ego! I used to think that it wasn't biblical and I would help God take care of Jack's … then I discovered it was part of what man is. Oops! Man must have gotten it from God! Sorry, Father.

Reverence your husband; admire and respect him. He will blossom, and what a wonderful fragrance it will bring to your relationship. Sweet! And, darlin', if you're thinking *I can't find anything good,* keep praying. There is something, and God will help you see it. When He does, thank your husband for whatever it is, without any other words less you lessen what you said. Then stand back, pray, and watch. Keep it up, and unless he's a total heathen, he'll become more and more your protector.

Enough said. Pray about all this. Start now. See you tomorrow.

DAY THREE

God-Rules FOR TODAY

Today we are going to the Torah—the law of God. From the beginning of its formation as a nation, Israel was to live under a theocracy. A theocracy means God rules! He's the law! And it's in His law that you will see His protection of a woman's sexuality.

You are going to look at quite a few verses from Leviticus 18—verses 6 to 30, but they are important as they spell out clearly what the Creator of sex has to say about how we are to behave sexually—what is right, what is wrong, how God feels about it, and the consequences that are to come if we disobey.

Read and mark the following Scripture carefully. There is considerable text to mark, but if you want to mark more than I suggest, feel free to do so. Be sure you mark the following, double underlining the references to *land* in green. It tells you where something is happening or to be done. Mark every reference to:

- *Women*
- *Blood relative*
- A *sexual activity*—uncovering nakedness, lying with someone, intercourse. You can simply use a big *S* if you want.
- *Defile*
- *Abomination, abominable*
- *Lewdness, perversion*
- *Land*

Uncovering Another's Nakedness

In the Hebrew, uncover the nakedness is *gala era* and is used most frequently for designating proscribed sexual activity. It occurs 24 times in Leviticus 18 and 20 in the expression "to uncover the shame," which denotes sexual intercourse in proscribed situations, usually incest. In many passages, then, it has the connotation "to shame."

Alongside of Leviticus 18 and 20 it occurs in the prophetic complaint that Israel has "uncovered her nakedness," a metaphor denoting that she threw off her loyalty to the Lord. Against this, the Lord or her former lovers will "expose the nakedness"—"to shame" of the faithless nation.[7]

LEVITICUS 18:6-30

[6] None of you shall approach any blood relative of his to uncover nakedness; I am the Lord.

[7] You shall not uncover the nakedness of your father, that is, the nakedness of your mother. She is your mother; you are not to uncover her nakedness.

[8] You shall not uncover the nakedness of your father's wife; it is your father's nakedness.

[9] The nakedness of your sister, either your father's daughter or your mother's daughter, whether born at home or born outside, their nakedness you shall not uncover.

[10] The nakedness of your son's daughter or your daughter's daughter, their nakedness you shall not uncover; for their nakedness is yours.

[11] The nakedness of your father's wife's daughter, born to your father, she is your sister, you shall not uncover her nakedness.

[12] You shall not uncover the nakedness of your father's sister; she is your father's blood relative.

[13] You shall not uncover the nakedness of your mother's sister, for she is your mother's blood relative.

[14] You shall not uncover the nakedness of your father's brother; you shall not approach his wife, she is your aunt.

[15] You shall not uncover the nakedness of your daughter-in-law; she is your son's wife, you shall not uncover her nakedness.

[16] You shall not uncover the nakedness of your brother's wife; it is your brother's nakedness.

[17] You shall not uncover the nakedness of a woman and of her daughter, nor shall you take her son's daughter or her daughter's daughter, to uncover her nakedness; they are blood relatives. It is lewdness.

[18] You shall not marry a woman in addition to her sister as a rival while she is alive, to uncover her nakedness.

[19] Also you shall not approach a woman to uncover her nakedness during her menstrual impurity.

²⁰ You shall not have intercourse with your neighbor's wife,
to be defiled with her.

²¹ You shall not give any of your offspring to offer them
to Molech, nor shall you profane the name of your God;
I am the LORD.

²² You shall not lie with a male as one lies with a female;
it is an abomination.

²³ Also you shall not have intercourse with any animal to be
defiled with it, nor shall any woman stand before an animal
to mate with it; it is a perversion.

²⁴ Do not defile yourselves by any of these things; for by all
these the nations which I am casting out before you have
become defiled.

²⁵ For the land has become defiled, therefore I have brought
its punishment upon it, so the land has spewed out its
inhabitants.

²⁶ But as for you, you are to keep My statutes and My judg-
ments and shall not do any of these abominations, neither
the native, nor the alien who sojourns among you

²⁷ (for the men of the land who have been before you have
done all these abominations, and the land has become
defiled);

²⁸ so that the land will not spew you out, should you defile it,
as it has spewed out the nation which has been before you.

²⁹ For whoever does any of these abominations, those persons
who do so shall be cut off from among their people.

³⁰ Thus you are to keep My charge, that you do not practice
any of the abominable customs which have been practiced
before you, so as not to defile yourselves with them; I am
the LORD your God.

Good job, faithful one! I am so proud of you for wanting to discover
truth for yourself and for being a thinking woman. Now, I want you
to read through these verses again. Take a few minutes and think about

what you have just read. This is the will of God! It is what God says. There's no mystery here, no hidden meaning. It's pretty plain, isn't it?

Reading the text again, use a blue pen and make notes in the margin of the Scriptures.
- You will find the laws grouped according to the kind of immorality it covers: incest, adultery, homosexuality, and bestiality. Note *where* these are mentioned in the margin of your book.
- Write down or underline the *who*—father, mother, sister, brother, neighbor, and so forth.
- Note in the margin *how* these transgressions affect the land.

Now read Deuteronomy 23:17-18. Mark the reference to *women* and mark any reference to *prostitution*.

DEUTERONOMY 23:17-18
¹⁷ None of the daughters of Israel shall be a cult prostitute, nor shall any of the sons of Israel be a cult prostitute.
¹⁸ You shall not bring the hire of a harlot or the wages of a dog into the house of the LORD your God for any votive offering, for both of these are an abomination to the LORD your God.

Prostitution is a lucrative business both in the United States and around the world. Millions of women and children are taken into it unwillingly where they are held as virtual slaves. They think they are going to another city or country to earn money to help support their families only to find they've become part of a prostitution business. They look as if they are willingly selling themselves on the streets and in public lobbies when in reality they are under the watchful eye of a menacing pimp.

Sometimes others willingly go into prostitution—or should I say *willfully* because very few enjoy the degradation. Rather, they choose prostitution because it provides the most money to support their children or family. Prostitution is rarely a job a person loves to have.

I am saying all of this, beloved, so you will have a better understanding of these women and seek to minister to them, not in word only but also in deeds.

Finally, I want us to look at Deuteronomy 22:5: "A woman shall not wear man's clothing, nor shall a man put on a woman's clothing; for whoever does these things is an abomination to the LORD your God." Many have used this verse to teach that a woman should not wear pants, but pants were modest and protective attire of women in biblical times in the Middle East.

If it doesn't refer to what is currently taught, to what might it be referring?

Well, this has been quite a day, hasn't it? Do you feel that you know and understand God a little better after looking at His Law?

What do you think the world would say about God's law?

To whose worldview will you hold when ideas clash?

Do you think you can compromise the Word of God to any degree? Explain your answer here.

Now, talk to God about what you have learned. As you do, do you think others ought to know these things? What are you going to do about it?

DAY FOUR

OUR SEXUALITY
PROTECTED

We're going to return to the Torah today. As a matter of fact, we're going to the Book of Leviticus again, but this time it's to take a look at the consequences of disobeying God in respect to what He deems abominations, lewdness, and perversion. As we do so, I want to remind you that we are looking at how God protects a woman's sexuality. How important is it?

> **Leviticus 20:7-24 is printed for you. As you read it aloud, mark the text as you did yesterday. Mark the references to:**
> - *Sexual immoralities of all kinds*—or the people who do them, such as adulterers
> - *Death*
> - *Bloodguiltiness*
> - *Bear their guilt, bear their sin*

LEVITICUS 20:7-24

7 You shall consecrate yourselves therefore and be holy, for I am the LORD your God.

8 You shall keep My statutes and practice them; I am the LORD who sanctifies you.

9 If there is anyone who curses his father or his mother, he shall surely be put to death; he has cursed his father or his mother, his bloodguiltiness is upon him.

10 If there is a man who commits adultery with another man's wife, one who commits adultery with his friend's wife, the adulterer and the adulteress shall surely be put to death.

11 If there is a man who lies with his father's wife, he has uncovered his father's nakedness; both of them shall surely be put to death, their bloodguiltiness is upon them.

¹² If there is a man who lies with his daughter-in-law, both of them shall surely be put to death; they have committed incest, their bloodguiltiness is upon them.

¹³ If there is a man who lies with a male as those who lie with a woman, both of them have committed a detestable act; they shall surely be put to death. Their bloodguiltiness is upon them.

¹⁴ If there is a man who marries a woman and her mother, it is immorality; both he and they shall be burned with fire, so that there will be no immorality in your midst.

¹⁵ If there is a man who lies with an animal, he shall surely be put to death; you shall also kill the animal.

¹⁶ If there is a woman who approaches any animal to mate with it, you shall kill the woman and the animal; they shall surely be put to death. Their bloodguiltiness is upon them.

¹⁷ If there is a man who takes his sister, his father's daughter or his mother's daughter, so that he sees her nakedness and she sees his nakedness, it is a disgrace; and they shall be cut off in the sight of the sons of their people. He has uncovered his sister's nakedness; he bears his guilt.

¹⁸ If there is a man who lies with a menstruous woman and uncovers her nakedness, he has laid bare her flow, and she has exposed the flow of her blood; thus both of them shall be cut off from among their people.

¹⁹ You shall also not uncover the nakedness of your mother's sister or of your father's sister, for such a one has made naked his blood relative; they will bear their guilt.

²⁰ If there is a man who lies with his uncle's wife he has uncovered his uncle's nakedness; they will bear their sin. They will die childless.

²¹ If there is a man who takes his brother's wife, it is abhorrent; he has uncovered his brother's nakedness. They will be childless.

²² You are therefore to keep all My statutes and all My ordinances and do them, so that the land to which I am bringing you to live will not spew you out.

²³ Moreover, you shall not follow the customs of the nation which I will drive out before you, for they did all these things, and therefore I have abhorred them.

²⁴ Hence I have said to you, "You are to possess their land, and I Myself will give it to you to possess it, a land flowing with milk and honey." I am the LORD your God, who has separated you from the peoples.

Now go back and read the text again. This time color-code or mark every reference to *the* LORD. When you finish, list what you learn about the Lord in this passage.

Finally, beloved of God, does this show you how precious your sexuality and its purity are to the Lord? What does such knowledge do to you?

By the way, has anyone told you recently that you are loved? I want to join God in saying it, but surely you know, don't you? If not, you are not believing God, and He so longs for you to believe Him.

What is your prayer today? Let it be your praise of worship to your omniscient Creator, your all-knowing God, your merciful Savior.

A PICTURE OF DANGER AND VULNERABILITY

When as a single you held your own and resisted sex outside of marriage, perhaps a man challenged you with a statement something like, "If you really loved me, you wouldn't make me wait" or "We'll eventually get married anyway. It's all right; it really is. We love each other."

Let me take you to the story of Amnon and Tamar, children of King David, and see what insight we can glean from this story God chose to record in His Word. As we look at it, I want you to look at it as both a woman and as a mother. This is a good story for you and your daughter to study and discuss together. You can become aware of your own vulnerabilities as women or the danger of being around men who do not fear God or who have a religion without a relationship with Him.

> 2 SAMUEL 13:1
> Now it was after this that Absalom the son of David had a beautiful sister whose name was Tamar, and Amnon the son of David loved her.

Let's pause for a moment and put a clock like this ⏰ over "after this," because it tells us when this incident is happening. The story of Amnon, Absalom, and Tamar follows David's adulterous relationship with Bathsheba, who was married to Uriah, one of David's valiant men. It follows the prophet Nathan's confrontation with David and his pronouncement of the consequence of David's sin.

It seems David had at least six wives when he took Bathsheba. Six wives—and seven children from these wives. He would have four by

Bathsheba and then nine more whose mothers' names we don't know. Talk about blended families!

Absalom and Tamar were born to David through Maacah, his fourth wife. Amnon was the son of Ahinoam, David's second wife. The text tells us Amnon loved his half-sister, Tamar. Go back and put a heart over the word *loved*.

2 SAMUEL 13:2
Amnon was so frustrated because of his sister Tamar that he made himself ill, for she was a virgin, and it seemed hard to Amnon to do anything to her.

Obviously Amnon was burning with desire, and he knew he could not take Tamar because she was a virgin. Either the man's conscience was holding him back or the virgins' isolation from the eligible young males made it impossible for him to get near her. Regardless, knowing Tamar sexually was all that was on Amnon's mind.

2 SAMUEL 13:3-4
3 But Amnon had a friend whose name was Jonadab, the son of Shimeah, David's brother; and Jonadab was a very shrewd man.
4 He said to him, "O son of the king, why are you so depressed morning after morning? Will you not tell me?" Then Amnon said to him, "I am in love with Tamar, the sister of my brother Absalom."

Have you ever been at a point where you can't shake your desire, you can't get *him* off your mind? You think of nothing else, no one else, imagining what it would be like to be together. In all probability as a woman you're not necessarily thinking about the actual act of sexual intercourse as much as a relationship, the romance of it all—being loved, being in love, being together, cherished, kissed, touched—the wonder of it all that you've tucked away with every romance novel, every movie.

Amnon's cousin and friend was shrewd. We know nothing about Jonadab except for the deadly advice he gave his cousin, advice that reveals his character—or lack thereof. From the first chapter of the book of Proverbs, Solomon would warn his son about men like Amnon. "My son, if sinners entice you, do not consent" (Prov. 1:10).

Later the apostle Paul would warn the Corinthians that evil companions corrupt good morals. Watch whose counsel you follow, my sister, because when all is said and done, you cannot pass the blame! With God you can never point the finger to someone else and say, "But they said it was all right, they made it possible, they suggested, they dared me." Hush. It won't stand in the court of heaven. But back to David.

> 2 SAMUEL 13:5-7
> ⁵ Jonadab then said to him, "Lie down on your bed and pretend to be ill; when your father comes to see you, say to him, 'Please let my sister Tamar come and give me some food to eat, and let her prepare the food in my sight, that I may see it and eat from her hand.' "
> ⁶ So Amnon lay down and pretended to be ill; when the king came to see him, Amnon said to the king, "Please let my sister Tamar come and make me a couple of cakes in my sight, that I may eat from her hand."
> ⁷ Then David sent to the house for Tamar, saying, "Go now to your brother Amnon's house, and prepare food for him."

Daddy wasn't thinking—and he ought to have been! He ought to have been on high alert after what happened in his own life with Bathsheba.

Why did Amnon specifically request Tamar?

Don't let your children blindside you. You weren't born yesterday. Surely you remember when you were entering puberty, or were a teen or college student. You are not over the hill, darling, even though they think you are. Stop and evaluate why your children or grandchildren are asking for the keys, checking out your schedule, telling you where they are going or not going, not staying home, skirting around your words of caution about a certain friend.

Think About Our Culture

- Think about the culture in which your children live. It's saturated with sex.
- It's amoral!
- We live in a culture that has had little exposure to the Word of God—especially the Old Testament. Some churches give less attention than they need to on maturing believers in the knowledge of God and equipping them for the work of ministry, as Ephesians 4 teaches us.
- Our culture today knows nothing of the fear of God!

Don't set up your children to fail. Do you know how many teens lose their virginity in their own homes? In *their* bedrooms? Our homes are supposed to be shelters, places of protection where we're safe from the world and all its lusts, where we are taught, nurtured, matured, and prepared to handle life.

Bedrooms ought to be off-limits for members of the opposite sex, as should dorm rooms and apartments. The rule ought to be that you are never in the home alone with someone of the opposite sex who's not a family member—and sometimes even there you have to be careful if the brother or sister has friends over. No parties without parental supervision.

In addition, parents ought to perform periodic reconnaissance missions at unexpected times.

I read of one mother who, walking through a bedroom in her home, saw her 16-year-old nephew under the sheets with her 10-year-old daughter. She didn't say a word but just kept walking. Several days later she threw an offhand statement at her daughter: "You'd better not be doing anything in bed." What kind of parenting is that? The sheet should have been jerked off immediately. "Flee from youthful lusts," Paul wrote Timothy, his son in the Lord (2 Tim. 2:22). Avoid the very appearance of evil.

> 2 SAMUEL 13:8
> So Tamar went to her brother Amnon's house, and he was lying down. And she took dough, kneaded it, made cakes in his sight, and baked the cakes.

And what was Amnon doing? Watching the folds of her dress cling to her body as she prepared his meal … dreaming of taking her to his bed … imagining what she would look like when—

> 2 SAMUEL 13:9
> She took the pan and dished them out before him, but he refused to eat. And Amnon said, "Have everyone go out from me." So everyone went out from him.

A man on death row—which was where Amnon unknowingly was headed—described the power of the lust of his eyes like this: "For me, seeing pornography was like lighting a fuse on a stick of dynamite; I became stimulated and had to gratify my urges or explode."[8]

> 2 SAMUEL 13:10
> Then Amnon said to Tamar, "Bring the food into the bedroom, that I may eat from your hand." So Tamar took the cakes which she had made and brought them into the bedroom to her brother Amnon.

Had it not occurred to Tamar what was happening? Did she not under-stand the lust that can overtake a man simply by watching and visualizing the taking of a woman? From the text, it seems that Tamar was innocent. Like many other women, she didn't understand the workings of a man sexually; she didn't recognize the trap that had been set for her.

The situation reminds me of a letter I read regarding a marriage that ended in divorce despite hope and expectation that the couple's marriage would be healed. But, finally she left—she just couldn't take it anymore.

Thirteen years she endured his infidelity, neglect, cruelty, drugs, alcohol: years in which she'd leave for several months and then come back to begin the cycle again, years of living off and on in a shelter with their children.

Then a newly divorced man showed up at church. No family of his own. Kind. Charming. He helped her and the children move from the shelter to a house and get her first car. The man had a lot of excess baggage, but he was there for her, giving her money for the divorce.

Yet all the time he was setting her up, luring her into his trap. Then when he felt it was safe, he made his move. He shared that he was so wounded, so disil-lusioned with women that the only way he could ever be gratified was to be his own image of a woman.

He vowed that if she didn't marry him, he would have the surgery he needed to look and act like a real woman—unless, of course, he could have her—then he wouldn't need to take that drastic step.

Of course you can read the handwriting on the wall. ... She discovered the man she married had been caught in the snare of pornography since the age of five and had lived in a fantasy world ever since. A world that is totally disgusting to her—yet she stays because "He said if I told anyone at church he would quit the church and disappear. I want to go to church for counseling, but I am afraid they will protect him and shun me since he's been in the church family for seven years, in their choir, and always seeking public attention from the staff."

"Come into my web," said the spider to the fly.

"But if I do, I think I'll die ... I think I'll die."

Beloved, what you're learning can help you help other women and enable your church to be a safe place for women who need such healing and acceptance and forgiveness. But let's find out what happened to Tamar. Keep observing what God teaches.

2 SAMUEL 13:11-13

11 When she brought them to him to eat, he took hold of her and said to her, "Come, lie with me, my sister."

12 But she answered him, "No, my brother, do not violate me, for such a thing is not done in Israel; do not do this disgraceful thing!

13 "As for me, where could I get rid of my reproach? And as for you, you will be like one of the fools in Israel. Now therefore, please speak to the king, for he will not withhold me from you."

Tamar did not reject Amnon. She just didn't want him to violate her or his reputation. Such behavior would be disgraceful. She knew—as did Amnon—that sex outside of marriage, sex apart from the covenant, is unacceptable in God's eyes. Their father had engaged in such behavior, and look at the shame it brought. How the enemies of God blasphemed the name of God!

So she suggested, "Wait. Let's go to our father the king. He understands. He will not withhold me from you. I'll be yours. I'm not rejecting you; I am just asking you to wait, to do what's right, to respect me, to not bring reproach on me."

Amnon loved Tamar—or at least that's what he thought. He even told Jonadab that he did. He had restrained his desires so much that he had made himself sick, because it seemed hard, cruel, wrong to violate the virgin he loved.

So what changed?

"Ohhhh, baby, baby . . . don't make me wait. If you love me, if you really love me, please don't make me wait."

"Each one is tempted when he's carried away by his own lust."

2 SAMUEL 13:14

However, he would not listen to her; since he was stronger
than she, he violated her and lay with her.

He violated her. The word *violated (anah)* means to depress, to bring down. Amnon forced himself on Tamar. He had taken her mentally; now he wanted her physically and he would not wait. He would satisfy his desire at the expense of her virginity, her reputation, and her welfare—and his own as well.

Sex outside of marriage is the most self-centered act anyone can perform. And though you may think you're acting in secret, in the dark, your sin is performed in the presence of a holy Trinity. The Father created you, the Son died for you, and the Spirit desires to live in you and give you the power to overcome every temptation.

2 SAMUEL 13:15

Then Amnon hated her with a very great hatred; for the hatred
with which he hated her was greater than the love with which
he had loved her. And Amnon said to her, "Get up, go away!"

Did you mark *love* again? And how would you mark *haste?* How about a heart again with a line through it, like this: ♡

In a matter of minutes—or did it only take seconds?—love turned to hate. Lust turned to disgust. *Disgust with whom, I wonder?*

Why did Amnon want Tamar, the dream of his life, to get up and go away? Where was the tenderness of love, the gratitude, and the delight that overwhelms a man or woman after they've made love? No matter how strong the desire, sex outside of marriage leaves a nagging guilt deep inside, an unexplainable dissatisfaction, a void that's still not filled.

God knows why. Remember, He's the manufacturer. He knows His "product." He knows what brings total satisfaction—and that abuse of His product brings only regret and loathing.

"GET UP! GO AWAY!"

Tamar has just been ravished! Violated! The blood of her virginity is on his sheets, and he orders *her* to get up and walk out of the bedroom, through the house, and out the door!

2 SAMUEL 13:16-18

[16] But she said to him, "No, because this wrong in sending me away is greater than the other that you have done to me!" Yet he would not listen to her.

[17] Then he called his young man who attended him and said, "Now throw this woman out of my presence, and lock the door behind her."

[18] Now she had on a long-sleeved garment; for in this manner the virgin daughters of the king dressed themselves in robes. Then his attendant took her out and locked the door behind her.

What incredible shame Amnon brought on Tamar! He was ill. Very ill. Sick with lust. In all probability Ammon treated Tamar like this because he loathed himself.

This is what happens to those, male or female, who cannot control their sexual desires. Deep down inside, they loath themselves. Conquered by their passions, they are slaves—victims—and they know it.

What happens when we are drawn away by our own desires and where does it lead? The story of Amnon and Tamar give us the flesh and blood illustration, and James's "in your face epistle" explains it. So let's finish with Amnon and Tamar and then go to James chapter 1.

2 SAMUEL 13:19

Tamar put ashes on her head, and tore her long-sleeved
garment which was on her; and she put her hand on
her head and went away, crying aloud as she went.

Ashes on Tamar's forehead were a sign of her mourning as she grieved her
loss. Tamar's virginity had been stolen and could never be returned.

2 SAMUEL 13:20

Then Absalom her brother said to her, "Has Amnon your
brother been with you? But now keep silent, my sister, he
is your brother; do not take this matter to heart." So Tamar
remained and was desolate in her brother Absalom's house.

Desolate. The Hebrew word God chose is *shamem,* and it comes from a
word that means "ruined." A brother's uncontrolled passion ruined the
life of his sister. How many men have ruined their blood relative's lives
by forcing themselves on a girl in the family, threatening her or her family
if she ever tells? What does God think about someone who would do
this to another? Do you think the perpetrator will go free and escape the
just judgment of God? Not according to God's Book! Numbers 32:23
assures us sure that our sins will find us out!

2 SAMUEL 13:21

Now when King David heard of all these matters, he was very
angry.

And rightly so! But what did David do about it? The Scripture seems to
speak through its silence. Apparently David failed as a father; he didn't
confront his children, deal with the issue, pronounce judgment, and
bring a just resolution. Had he learned nothing from Nathan? Was he
silent because of a guilty conscience? Were his thoughts consumed with
his own remorse? "How can I say anything? Look at what I've done!"

Oh beloved, sinning against God, failing God does not mean that we
can never open our mouths again or call sin by name. Our past personal

sin does not negate our responsibility to deal with sin when it occurs in the family.

Sin is always to be dealt with according to the Word of God, never on the basis of our righteousness or lack of it! If we ignore it, the wound will fester and more damage will be done in the process. This is why every child molester needs to be exposed and made to face the just consequences of his or her sin. If not, the sin will continue and others will suffer. Every immoral failure within the leadership of the church must be dealt with; it is not to be hidden so the person can do it again.

David should have followed the precepts of God we studied in Deuteronomy 22, the guidelines that set forth what is to be done. Amnon should have married his sister. And maybe in doing what was right, noble, and good, Amnon's love for Tamar would have been restored.

But as far as we know, the situation was never dealt with biblically.

2 SAMUEL 13:22
But Absalom did not speak to Amnon either good or bad;
for Absalom hated Amnon because he had violated his sister
Tamar.

Two years later Absalom killed Amnon. And in reality, David lost two sons: Amnon and Absalom. Bitterness defiles and destroys. Death in some form always follows sin.

Let's look at James 1:13-17. As you read these verses aloud, mark every reference to being tempted or enticed. You can use a fishhook like this if ⎰ you like. Also mark *death* as you have done before.

JAMES 1:13-17
[13] Let no one say when he is tempted, "I am being tempted by God"; for God cannot be tempted by evil, and He Himself does not tempt anyone.
[14] But each one is tempted when he is carried away and enticed by his own lust.

¹⁵ Then when lust has conceived, it gives birth to sin;
   and when sin is accomplished, it brings forth death.
¹⁶ Do not be deceived, my beloved brethren.
¹⁷ Every good thing bestowed and every perfect gift is
   from above, coming down from the Father of lights,
   with whom there is no variation or shifting shadow.

Now, read it again; this time mark:
   • **References to** *sin.* **Color it brown, or put a scarlet** *S*
     over it.
   • **The references to** *God.*

So often, when a person sins sexually, it seems easy to say, "I just couldn't
help it! The desire was overwhelming. I'm sure you understand and God
understands. After all, He made me the way I am!" But is that true?

What does God say? What do you learn from marking
tempted **and** *enticed?*

What do you learn about sin? Is temptation the same as sin?
This is a very important question, and you need to make sure
you know what God says. Read the text carefully and write out
your answer.

What about death? What do you learn?

Now, according to this passage, is it a sin to be tempted?

Without reading any thoughts into Amnon's mind or projecting anything into the story, when, according to 2 Samuel and James I, did Amnon sin?

What died as a result of Amnon's unchecked lust, his yielding to temptation?

The Greek word translated *enticed* in James I:14 is quite a picturesque word. It's a term used in hunting for setting a trap and in fishing for baiting a hook to lure a fish out from under a rock. I am married to a fisherman, and if there's one thing I know from picking out fishing magazines for him, it's that fish love to hang out under rocks.

And who is our Rock, beneath whose shadow we need to hide? You got it! It's God, whose name is Cur—Rock! We're to hide in the cleft of the Rock, in the shelter of our God and stay there.

Do you think this might be why the Devil took up fishing? He knows he can never have us again as his own, but he surely desires to wipe us out, to lure us from the Rock and get us to swallow his bait. One of the most powerful and successful lures in his tackle box is sex. The Devil is an expert when it comes to threading that worm on his hook, leaving just enough bait wiggling to get our attention.

Sex successfully lured the family of King David!

- David slept with Bathsheba—another man's wife. He confessed and was forgiven but paid fourfold.
- Amnon raped his half-sister Tamar and was killed by Tamar's brother Absalom.
- Absalom, in a bitter quest for his father's throne, eventually slept with his father's concubines in full view of Israel and died hanging by his hair from a tree, speared by David's general Joab.

"Be sure your sin will find you out!" It's been quite a week, hasn't it? Is your head spinning?

Take a few minutes and look at what you studied each day this week. Jot some thoughts down here.

Day 1

Day 2

Day 3

Day 4

Today—Day 5

Now, is man to be a protector or a predator? If he acts as a predator toward you, are you to blame? Is something wrong with you? NO! Do *not* take this guilt on yourself. Do not believe a lie. If he acts as a predator, it is because something is wrong with him. You have been misused and God will act as your protector; the man's sin will not go unjudged.

Viewer Guide
SESSION 4

MAN: PREDATOR OR PROTECTOR?

Gala era
  Gala: To show something normally concealed
  Era: Laid bare or naked

Woman is to be _____ for who she is.

Through Jesus, man who was a predator can be _____ into a protector.

He ought to want to _____ her, protect her.

God has ordained for us to live like _____.

God has ordained for Jesus to be the _____.

THE

Seductress

(AND HOW NOT TO BE ONE)

Her words are seductive, her speech suggestive. Nothing is private, even the most intimate of issues. It's easy to spot a seductress; simply watch her eyes. You might think it a game to seduce a man with your eyes; but if you do, know that you will answer to God.

Beloved, study well the truths in your homework this week. Hide them in your heart, for they will tie you to the mast when the storms of temptation blow—or help you choose a wise course when you see a seductress coming onto the path of your husband or son. Many a wise wife has rescued her husband from a woman who would destroy him.

THIS WEEK, THROUGH YOUR
HOME STUDY, YOU WILL:

grow in your love for studying the Bible

learn how a woman's appearance and behavior
can be both seductive and destructive to a man

acknowledge the consequences of sexual sins,
especially adultery

commit to a life of faithfulness and purity

DAY ONE

Our Culture
SEDUCES

This week we must take a careful look at ourselves. We live in a culture more absorbed with our bodies than our character—and we're suffering dire consequences as a result.

Society tells us that who we are is not as important as how we appear. While this is not accurate, we often allow our identity and self-esteem to be found in the way we look. We want to be hot, to be sexy! Reflect on how sitcoms, movies, and the lives of the stars flaunt sex outside of marriage! Being rich and successful and involved in a passionate relationship seems foremost on people's minds—from teens on up.

Although God clearly sets forth in His Book that marriage is the door to sex, today's culture considers sex the door to love and then, once you've been "test driven" and passed the road test, to marriage.

What does God teach us about the seductress, the adulteress, and those who permit themselves to be seduced by her? Notice I said, "permit"—for according to God there is no excuse. Let's see what the Word of God has to say so we aren't seduced by the culture and find ourselves in the role of a seductress.

PRACTICAL WISDOM FOR LIFE

The beauty of a woman's sexuality can be the destruction of a man if the woman misuses what God has given her. Thus God moved King Solomon with others to write Proverbs, a book that contains practical wisdom for everyday life issues. Among them are warnings about the "strange woman"—translated "adulteress" in the New American Standard Bible but footnoted as literally "strange woman."

Although we have already looked at Proverbs 5:15-21 it will be good to look at it again in the context of the whole of Proverbs 5. God's Word is a living word that we can never exhaust nor grow weary of!

Read aloud Proverbs 5:1-23 and don't miss who Solomon addressed. When you finish, I'll have things for you to mark.

PROVERBS 5:1-23

¹ My son, give attention to my wisdom,
   Incline your ear to my understanding;
² That you may observe discretion
   And your lips may reserve knowledge.
³ For the lips of an adulteress drip honey
   And smoother than oil is her speech;
⁴ But in the end she is bitter as wormwood,
   Sharp as a two-edged sword.
⁵ Her feet go down to death,
   Her steps take hold of Sheol.
⁶ She does not ponder the path of life;
   Her ways are unstable, she does not know it.
⁷ Now then, my sons, listen to me
   And do not depart from the words of my mouth.
⁸ Keep your way far from her
   And do not go near the door of her house,
⁹ Or you will give your vigor to others
   And your years to the cruel one;
¹⁰ And strangers will be filled with your strength
   And your hard-earned goods will go to the house
   of an alien;
¹¹ And you groan at your final end,
   When your flesh and your body are consumed;
¹² And you say, "How I have hated instruction!
   And my heart spurned reproof!
¹³ "I have not listened to the voice of my teachers,
   Nor inclined my ear to my instructors!
¹⁴ "I was almost in utter ruin
   In the midst of the assembly and congregation."
¹⁵ Drink water from your own cistern
   And fresh water from your own well.

16 Should your springs be dispersed abroad,
   Streams of water in the streets?
17 Let them be yours alone
   And not for strangers with you.
18 Let your fountain be blessed,
   And rejoice in the wife of your youth.
19 As a loving hind and a graceful doe,
   Let her breasts satisfy you at all times;
   Be exhilarated always with her love.
20 For why should you, my son, be exhilarated with an adulteress
   And embrace the bosom of a foreigner?
21 For the ways of a man are before the eyes of the LORD,
   And He watches all his paths.
22 His own iniquities will capture the wicked,
   And he will be held with the cords of his sin.
23 He will die for lack of instruction,
   And in the greatness of his folly he will go astray.

Good! Now read it again and color-code the following:
   • every reference to the adulteress (strange woman),
     including all the pronouns
   • every reference to the son(s)—every *you, your*
   • every reference to *death* using a black tombstone

Now list what you learned about the adulteress and the son.

THE ADULTERESS   THE SON

This kind of woman is strange because, as you can see, she is not godly. Knowing her characteristics will help you not only examine yourself but also watch that you don't see these attributes in your daughter.

And, if you are a mother to sons, have grandsons, or work with young men, you are gaining valuable information they need to know. Our three sons were not allowed to date until they were 16 and could spot a strange woman. We didn't want any dumb men—one who is seduced by a strange woman!

This is enough for today. Let's take what we've learned from the Father's Book and talk to our Father. Review the list on the adulteress and ask God to show you any areas of weakness in your life that would keep you from the beauty of His purity. As you do, please also pray for a return to a desire for purity among women, a moving of the Spirit of God upon the women on this nation that will bring an awareness of God and a conviction of sin.

DAY TWO

A WOMAN ON THE PROWL

Although merely a tale from Greek mythology, *The Odyssey*, the Sirens' song tells us of an age-old battle of the flesh that rages within every human heart. For the Greeks, who didn't know the Word of God, it served as a warning, much like the strange women of the Book of Proverbs served the nation of Israel. Both Jews and Greeks are under sin's power until Jesus Christ sets us free. (See John 8:34,36; Rom. 3:9-18.)

The song of the Sirens was carried by the wind, skimmed the surface of the sea, was captured in the sails of the ship, and lured many a captain and his sailors to change their charted courses. Powerless to resist the Sirens' mesmerizing song, the bewitched men set their sails for the Sirens' shore. Beneath the surface of the sparkling waters dancing so gaily at the island's shore lay jagged rocks. Shipwreck was inevitable, yet some might wonder who would ever want to leave the Sirens' island anyway! Blinded by lust, they didn't realize that countless sailors like themselves had crashed on the rocky shores, only to be devoured by the Sirens. Underneath the Sirens' seductive attire was a cannibal appetite that savagely consumed their victims' flesh.

Circe, the enchantress with whom Odysseus (also called Ulysses) had just had an affair, warned him as he set a course for Ithaca to sail far around the island, lest he meet his doom in the Sirens' song. His curiosity awakened, Odysseus conceived another plan. As they neared the island, he ordered his sailors to fill their ears with wax to prevent being seduced by the Sirens. But Odysseus, longing just to hear their glorious voices, had another plan for himself. There would be no wax in his ears; instead, he instructed his crew to lash him to the mast of the ship, warning that no matter how fervently he pled with them they were not to untie him until they were far from the shores of the Sirens' island.

How right Circe was; how wise Odysseus was to listen. The song of the Sirens was so seductive his death was certain if he could have freed himself from the straps that bound him.

We are about to see that God has even more to say about "the siren" in Proverbs 6 and 7, obviously a matter of great concern!

Let's observe how God moves into the warning about the evil woman. Read the following verses aloud.

PROVERBS 6:20-24

[20] My son, observe the commandment of your father
   And do not forsake the teaching of your mother;
[21] Bind them continually on your heart;
   Tie them around your neck.
[22] When you walk about, they will guide you;
   When you sleep, they will watch over you;
   And when you awake, they will talk to you.

23 For the commandment is a lamp and the teaching is light;
And reproofs for discipline are the way of life
24 To keep you from the evil woman,
From the smooth tongue of the adulteress.

Read it again and ask **the 5 W's and an H: who** is speaking? To **whom,** about **what, when** is it happening or **when** is it to be done, **where** is it going to happen, **why** is it being said and **why** will it happen, and **how** is it to be done? See how many of these questions you can answer from the text.

Write your observations below. This is a good exercise as it helps you develop skills of observation.

The commandments of this son's father and mother were not frivolous orders tossed at their son without purpose; they were words that would keep him from shipwrecking his life! The son of the king was to continually bind these teachings upon his heart and tie them around his neck. These truths would provide direction, give him instruction, and protect him. If he would listen and obey, he would avoid the snare of the Sirens' song—the strong lure of temptation, the passion of his flesh, the cause of the destruction of young and old, small and great, naive and wise.

The father knows a man's eyes cannot help but see and then beckon the mind to imagine, the flesh to touch, to taste, to feel, to know—and he wanted to protect his son from the inevitable ruin that would follow such seduction. The wise father went on to say in Proverbs 6:25-26: "Do not desire her beauty in your heart, Nor let her capture you with her eyelids. For on account of a harlot one is reduced to a loaf of bread, And an adulteress hunts for the precious life."

An adulteress! A harlot! Mark every reference to her in the verses you just read (Prov. 6:20-24).

This is a woman on the hunt when God meant man to be the hunter. This is a woman who is skilled at seduction, calling him to her shores, luring him into her snare, taking captive her prey, and devouring all of his substance.

She would destroy that which would distinguish him as a man of character She would destroy one whose life was worthy to be imitated, whose sons would want to walk in his footsteps and whose daughters would delight in his moral strength and bask in the security of his integrity. In exchange for compromise of his integrity, this siren would bankrupt him of godlikeness, reducing his worth to the price of a loaf of bread.

This story, shared by a couple who leads Precept studies in their church in Canada, illustrates well the hunt of the adulteress.

> Their 17-year-old son and his buddies went to spend a day at Canada's Wonderland—a version of our Disney World in the USA. As they waited in line a young girl of about 16 struck up a conversation with the boys and then hung out with them the rest of the day. The girl found out only their son's name and the city he was from—nothing more. Yet the following Saturday she stood at their front door, ringing the doorbell. She had ridden the bus 50 miles to spend the day with their son. The entire family was in shock, but none more so than their son.
>
> She was dressed, as Proverbs says, in "the attire of a harlot"—a short cropped top, deep neckline, and tight jeans. Wanting to be kind and not rude to her and hesitant to turn her away, they spent an awkward day with her as a family and then took her to the bus station.
>
> A week later as my friend sorted the mail, she noticed a letter addressed to her son from their visitor. My friend said, "Kay, as I held the letter in my hand,

I knew that there was a condom inside the envelope. I prayed about how to approach my son as I knew he would be horrified when he opened it. When he got home, I told him a letter had come in the mail from this girl and that I just knew that it would have a condom inside. I just wanted to warn him. When he opened the letter, there was a colorful condom almost like Mickey Mouse with a note inside saying she was sending this in preparation for her next visit. My son was embarrassed to death—until this point in his life he had never seen a condom up close and personal."

When you read a story like this, you have a tendency to think—*But how many times would something like this ever happen again? How many women are on the hunt?* Unless you are in touch with the world or out in the workplace, you don't understand there are far more than we realize. Many a man will tell you if he wants sex, it's easy to get. No problem. There are more available women out there than you conjure in your mind. Women on the prowl. They write men notes, show up unexpectedly, call the house, and make it known just how available they are.

Oh, listen to the wisdom of Solomon—but don't follow his example. Solomon himself did not stay tied to the masthead of God—"he had seven hundred wives, princesses, and three hundred concubines, and his wives turned his heart away ... after other gods ... Solomon did what was evil in the sight of the LORD" (1 Kings 11:3-4,6). The adulteress ruins a man, destroys the family, and contributes to the demoralization of a nation.

Oh, dear one—God forbid that we should be such women. I was before I was saved at the age of 29. But the old Kay died on July 16, 1963. She no longer exists (see Rom. 6 and 2 Cor. 5:17). Yet because of my past, for many years I had to fight some "strange woman" temptations. But I knew where to run and what to do, and the Word of God and the Spirit of God contained and sustained me. And it can be the same for you, precious one. You can be a woman of excellence. But let's continue with Proverbs 6.

Color-code the following references to the man and the woman all the way through the text as you did yesterday.

And remember, although this is directed to Solomon's son, the street runs two ways! Watch the cooperative woman—the seductress and how she brings down a man. Discuss it with your husband so he won't be naive and ensnared. Teach it to your sons and daughters.

PROVERBS 6:27-35

27 Can a man take fire in his bosom
   And his clothes not be burned?
28 Or can a man walk on hot coals
   And his feet not be scorched?
29 So is the one who goes in to his neighbor's wife;
   Whoever touches her will not go unpunished.
30 Men do not despise a thief if he steals
   To satisfy himself when he is hungry;
31 But when he is found, he must repay sevenfold;
   He must give all the substance of his house.
32 The one who commits adultery with a woman
   is lacking sense;
   He who would destroy himself does it.
33 Wounds and disgrace he will find,
   And his reproach will not be blotted out.
34 For jealousy enrages a man,
   And he will not spare in the day of vengeance.
35 He will not accept any ransom,
   Nor will he be satisfied though you give many gifts.

Read the last verse again and think of the pain you will bring to your husband if you are unfaithful to him. He may forgive your act of infidelity, but according to this passage it will be a battle in his mind.

If you are being tempted, lured by an attraction to a man who is not your husband, or if you are a single woman who is attracted to a married man—do not go there. I guarantee it will not be worth the guilt and remorse that will come. No matter how much your heart may break, "fornicators and adulterers God will judge" (Heb. 13:4). He's the One who said it, and He watches over His Word to perform it! Judgment is inevitable and will come in time. You will not escape. You cannot escape because God is righteous.

DAY THREE

STRANGE WOMEN AND DUMB MEN

When you read Proverbs 7, it is obvious that the Spirit of God prods Solomon to continue binding his son to the masthead of God's Word, securing him with truth so that he might not give in to the Sirens' song. He's saying, "Let me tell you what I saw, what happened, that you might not walk the same path."

As you read on in chapter 7—aloud—continue color-coding references to the man and to the seductress—the adulteress. Watch for contrasting images (life and death, and so forth).

PROVERBS 7:1-10

¹ My son, keep my words
   And treasure my commandments within you.
² Keep my commandments and live,
   And my teaching as the apple of your eye.
³ Bind them on your fingers;
   Write them on the tablet of your heart.
⁴ Say to wisdom, "You are my sister,"
   And call understanding your intimate friend;

⁵ That they may keep you from an adulteress,
   From the foreigner who flatters with her words.
⁶ For at the window of my house
   I looked out through my lattice,
⁷ And I saw among the naive,
   And discerned among the youths
      A young man lacking sense,
⁸ Passing through the street near her corner;
   And he takes the way to her house,
⁹ In the twilight, in the evening,
   In the middle of the night and in the darkness.

Take a good look at this man. List what you observe so far.

WATCH OUT FOR BOTH!

I am sure you saw it. Here is a man who lacked sense, who (no matter how old he was) wouldn't flee his youthful lusts. He was a man who put himself in the path of temptation. A temptress lives in the neighborhood. Don't think the darkness can hide either of you. The darkness is not dark to God. The night is as bright as the day. Darkness and light are alike to Him (Ps. 139:11-12).

PROVERBS 7:10-12

¹⁰ And behold, a woman comes to meet him,
   Dressed as a harlot and cunning of heart.
¹¹ She is boisterous and rebellious,
   Her feet do not remain at home;
¹² She is now in the streets, now in the squares,
   And lurks by every corner.

As a woman you can understand what she is doing, can't you? She's on the hunt. Have you done the same thing? Before I was a Christian, when I was a single mother looking for a husband, I did. My intention was not to bed the man, just to attract him and make him want to bed me—although I would have said no. Believe me, as a single gal I knew where the man would be and I arranged to be there accidentally on purpose. And when I got there I intended to look as good as I could—as attractive and seductive as I could. I wanted to be sexy!

What about you? Do you love the look you see in the mirror as you think, *I've still got it—and I'm going to flaunt it?* Single or married, what message does your attire send? We will talk more about it tomorrow. Just think about it between now and then—and if you have a daughter or a single sister, look at her. What message is she sending?

PROVERBS 7:13-21

¹³ So she seizes him and kisses him
   And with a brazen face she says to him:
¹⁴ "I was due to offer peace offerings;
   Today I have paid my vows.
¹⁵ "Therefore I have come out to meet you,
   To seek your presence earnestly, and I have found you.
¹⁶ "I have spread my couch with coverings,
   With colored linens of Egypt.
¹⁷ "I have sprinkled my bed
   With myrrh, aloes and cinnamon.
¹⁸ "Come, let us drink our fill of love until morning;
   Let us delight ourselves with caresses.

¹⁹ "For my husband is not at home,
  He has gone on a long journey;
²⁰ He has taken a bag of money with him,
  At the full moon he will come home."
²¹ With her many persuasions she entices him;
  With her flattering lips she seduces him.

Single or married friend—are your conversations with men tainted with innuendos? Do you flirt? Seduce with your words? Maybe you are lonely, desperate for companionship or affirmation as a woman. Do you long for romance but opt to "play it safe" on the Internet? Do you think that no one will know or that you can safely engage in seductive conversations online?

You are wrong, my dear. Four always know. The omniscient, omnipresent Father; the Son; the Holy Spirit—and of course, you!

PROVERBS 7:22-23
²² Suddenly he follows her
  As an ox goes to the slaughter,
  Or as one in fetters to the discipline of a fool,
²³ Until an arrow pierces through his liver;
  As a bird hastens to the snare,
  So he does not know that it will cost him his life.

FROM INNOCENT BEGINNINGS

It began with an e-mail, then Internet pornography, and then chat rooms. Until then, no one knew. Then came the invitation to meet. At first he resisted, but the invitation came again. He went and left feeling dirty. Now she knew, but he wouldn't contact her again. His secret was safe.

Then another invitation came, this time from another woman. He went, and it became an affair that ended his marriage. He lost his wife but surely not the children. They were his life. Then came another e-mail, this one from his 19-year-old daughter:

"I cannot comprehend the sincerity of anything you say anymore, Dad. You say that you love me, yet you knowingly hurt both our family and me. ... I am learning that words are a cheap commodity. ...

"I am angry with you for living a life of deception and for going against everything you have ever taught me to be true and right. I disrespect you as a man, a husband, and as a father. You are a coward for not being willing to sacrifice something for the love of your own children. More than anything, I pity you. I pity you for throwing your life away for lust. You had every earthly thing a man could ever dream of: a loving family, two adoring children, a wonderful job, respect in our community, and all the possessions you could ever want. Yet you had a void in your life. Instead of filling that void with Christ, you allowed sin to fill it. You are caught inside a cloud of deception. I hurt for you because I know that one day you will look back at your life and realize all that you lost ... for nothing. And I am afraid for you because I know that God will deal with your sin in His time and that it will be far worse than any earthly punishment or grief you could encounter. You are in a dangerous position by not fearing the Lord. ...

"As disappointed and upset as I am, I will not cease to pray for you. I will pray that God will soften your heart. I will pray that you will not find the true peace or contentment until you are right with God. I will pray that one day, before we die, you will have a change of heart and lifestyle and that our relationship can be renewed. I will pray that, in time, God will grant me the grace to forgive you.[1]

I wonder if the woman who had an affair with this married man realized what she did to his family? To his wife? I know I didn't when—before I was saved—I fell in love with Jim. I assumed he was single when I met him, but I never asked. When I found out he was married, I was so in love with him I didn't care. Nor did the affair stop when I found out his wife was pregnant with their sixth child!

Then, in the grace of God, the conviction of sin came upon this lost woman who was so desperately looking for love. Not too long after that I called his wife and met with her. We discovered she had found out about us. After two years I ended an affair with a man I deeply loved like no other.

But that's not the end of the story. Jim found me about a year after I was saved. I was a student in Bible school but feeling very lonely trying to raise my two sons, earn enough money to support us, and make good grades. When the phone rang and I heard him say "Kay," I knew it was Jim. But this time, although I longed just to see him face-to-face one more time, I was able to say no, give him the gospel, and tell him never to contact me again.

> PROVERBS 7:24-27
> [24] My sons, listen to me,
>   And pay attention to the words of my mouth.
> [25] Do not let your heart turn aside to her ways,
>   Do not stray into her paths.
> [26] For many are the victims she has cast down,
>   And numerous are all her slain.
> [27] Her house is the way to Sheol,
>   Descending to the chambers of death.

Read that last verse again—did you mark the reference to the strange woman, the adulteress? Oh, woman of God's creation, don't let your house be the way to the grave! God forbid that you should be an instrument of death in a man's life!

If you say you cannot help yourself—that you are melted butter in the heat of passion, that you can't risk letting him go, that you never hear

God's voice calling you away from temptation—could it possibly be that you are not His child? Maybe you have a religion but not a relationship. God does not want you to be deceived. Remember what we observed in 1 Corinthians 6:9-10? "Do not be deceived; neither fornicators, nor idolaters, nor adulterers, nor effeminate, nor homosexuals, nor thieves, nor the covetous, nor drunkards, nor revilers, nor swindlers, will inherit the kingdom of God."

If this is what you are, if this is your character, your lifestyle, then you are lost. You will self-destruct. But if you want out, if you want to change, God will change you. He can take up residence within you, bringing His Son and His Spirit. All you have to do is ask God to move in, and He will give you the wisdom and power to say no to sin and to walk away in the power of the Holy Spirit.

I want to make sure you do not miss what Proverbs 7 says about the strange woman and the naive (dumb) man! Read through the text you've marked and list your observations.

THE ADULTERESS   THE NAIVE MAN

SPOTTING A SEDUCTRESS

Many a wise woman has rescued her man from a woman who would destroy him. Men can be naive—oblivious to her wiles—but another woman often reads them well.

Her words are seductive, her speech suggestive. No propriety. Romance is a lost art, a discarded social grace. Nothing is private anymore, not even the most intimate of issues. There is no modesty nor delicacy of speech. Women's words are brazen, blunt, and, unfortunately, as it says in the Book of Jeremiah, we no longer blush. Nothing is sacred—especially not sex, even though God meant it to be.

I can easily spot a seductress; I simply watch her eyes, especially around men. A woman's eyes are the windows of her soul, and they'll tell you much about what is inside. You might think it a game to seduce a man merely with your eyes, but if you do, my dear, you will answer to God. It's a fearful thing to fall into the hands of the living God.

Oh girls, do you realize that in our aggressiveness we rob men of their masculinity? They love the hunt, the conquest! There's an innate nobility in the hearts of many men—the desire to protect, to cherish, to care for a woman as the weaker sex—and we have almost made it extinct. This strange woman bought into a lie; she thought being sexy, seducing man after man, demonstrated her power and proved her femininity.

This woman is not a "home body." She wants to be out there on the streets, in the middle of the action. She's loud and boisterous; she is going to be heard, noticed! There's a brazenness about her sexuality. Her goal is to bed the man! Why? It could be that the poor woman craves love and thinks it will come by giving herself away. Or possibly she hates herself, feels worthless, and expects to be used. Maybe she was inducted into this life because of the sexual abuse she suffered as a child or as a young woman. Maybe she ended up there because of alcohol, drugs, or poverty. There can be a dozen different reasons, but all of them are wrong and my heart aches for her. I want to take her in my arms, call her beloved, tell her she is precious to God and that this is not what God intends for her, that this is not how a woman finds fulfillment.

Proverbs 5:6 tells us she is not a thinking woman, that she lives for the present or is entangled by her past. "She does not ponder the path of life; her ways are unstable, she does not know it." Giving away your body for anything other than marriage leads to an empty, lonely, dissatisfying, frustrating life.

What is her future? What will she have left when her beauty fades—and she's forgotten or missed the joys God intended for woman? When she's replaced by the next available generation? When she can no longer sing the Sirens' song?

WHO CAN FIND A VIRTUOUS WOMAN?

Oh, precious one, Jesus can make you a virtuous woman if you will only come to Him, even as...

- the Samaritan woman who had five husbands and was living with a man
- Mary Magdalene who had seventy demons, all cast out by Jesus
- the woman who sinned much and came to wash Jesus' feet with her tears and found her sins forgiven
- I came to Him.

Your worth is above rubies; God paid for you with the life of His Son. What more could He do to prove His love to you, precious one?

There's another song you and I should be listening for and sharing with others. The myth of the Sirens' song continues in the story of Jason, a character of Greek mythology who was brought up and educated by the centaur Chiron. Jason, too, heard the Sirens' song as he sailed his ship, the Argo, past the infamous island of destruction. Unlike Odysseus, however, Jason would neither plug the ears of his men, the Argonauts, nor bind himself or them to the ship's mast. Instead, Jason commanded Orpheus, a musician of extraordinary talent, to play his music—the most beautiful music he had ever created. As they sailed past the island, the men never heard the Sirens' song wafting toward them on the waves of the sea. Instead, they were enraptured by the transcendent beauty of another's music.

Listen, my friend, to God's song: "The LORD will command His lovingkindness in the daytime; And His song will be with me in the night, a prayer to the God of my life" (Ps. 42:8). "Behold, God is my salvation, I will trust and not be afraid; For the LORD GOD is my strength and song, And He has become my salvation" (Isa. 12:2). *His* song transcends all others.

DAY FOUR

OUR CHOICES CAN
SHIPWRECK US

We often forget—or we hope and pray—there won't be consequences to our behavior, our choices. Believe me, darling, there will be consequences even under the covenant of grace. Some think God's grace gives us a license to sin, but it doesn't! Rather, it gives us the power not to sin because it gives us the gift of the Spirit. When we walk in the Spirit we will not fulfill the desires of the flesh. Thus God tells us that judgment begins at the house of God, and He holds His children to a very high standard. Not only does God call us to righteousness but He also gives us the power to be righteous.

The beauty of our sexuality is to be guarded and used wisely. And this is what I want us to study today. We need to understand the consequences of misusing our sexuality.

When you studied Proverbs 6 did you notice verse 33: "wounds and disgrace will he find, and his reproach will not be blotted out"? Wounds and disgrace are the consequences of committing adultery with the adulteress.

The title *adulteress* describes the character of this woman; it pegs her as a woman who has known more than one man! This is her pattern, her lifestyle. The word *wounds* is from the Hebrew word *nega* meaning stroke, plague, disease. *Nega* comes from *naga*, which essentially means "to touch" or "that which pertains when one thing or person physically contacts another." Interesting, isn't it? These words pertain to STDs—sexually transmitted diseases—that plague women and men all over the world.

Reason with me: If the man gets wounds—where did they come from? From the woman! And where did she get them? From a man she had sex with! According to former U. S. Surgeon General Dr. C. Everett Koop, "When you have sex with someone, you are having sex with everyone they have had sex with for the last ten years, and everyone they and their partners have had sex with for the last ten years." [2]

> **Look at I Corinthians 6:18 again. As you read the verse, see if it references "reaping what you sow." In other words, do consequences to disobedience exist? If so, underline the consequences as you read.**
>> "Flee immorality. Every other sin that a man commits is outside the body, but the immoral man sins against his own body."

What do you think "sins against his own body" means? Before you answer, look at Romans 1:25-27 for additional insight. This passage deals with God's judgment on those who do not honor Him as God but become vain in their imaginations.

- **Color in a distinctive way the references to** *they, them, their.*
- **Distinguish the women and men by coloring them as you have done before.**
- **Underline anything that indicates consequences to actions.**

ROMANS 1:25-27

[25] For they exchanged the truth of God for a lie, and worshiped and served the creature rather than the Creator, who is blessed forever. Amen.

[26] For this reason God gave them over to degrading passions; for their women exchanged the natural function for that which is unnatural,

[27] and in the same way also the men abandoned the natural function of the woman and burned in their desire toward one another, men with men committing indecent acts and receiving in their own persons the due penalty of their error.

What did you learn from these verses in I Corinthians and Romans 1? Where are the consequences experienced or felt?

Look at Hebrews 13:4. Read the verse and once again underline anything that indicates there is a consequence when we break God's commandments.

"Marriage is to be held in honor among all, and the marriage bed is to be undefiled; for fornicators and adulterers God will judge."

What is the consequence, who will reap it, and why?

God has made it clear: Misusing what God has given us—in adultery, fornication, and sexual sin—is displeasing to God and calls for His judgment. Men and women are stewards of their sexuality. God is not partial, and He allows no exemptions. He cannot overlook sin. It goes against His character and violates His righteousness.

CONSEQUENCES OF ADULTERY

Keep in mind, beloved, adultery carries some very real consequences.

First, adultery breaks a covenant and invites God's judgment. Our sin is against the Almighty, who "has been a witness between you and the wife of your youth, against whom you have dealt treacherously, though she is your companion and your wife by covenant" (Mal. 2:14).

King David is a perfect illustration of this outcome. Although he eventually confessed his sin of adultery with Bathsheba and his strategy for getting rid of her husband Uriah, he still had to bear the consequences. And while we might think that David's confession was enough, it wasn't.

Sin has become too common and grace too cheap. When we think of grace, we often think of "getting off scot-free," with no consequences. We think a simple "I'm sorry, God" will turn everything the way it was before. But that's not grace. Grace is not license to sin; rather, it is power to keep you from sin.

Grace is favor; it is everything that God has made available to us, but it doesn't remove the consequences. You can have sexual intercourse and then tell God you are sorry, and in grace God will forgive you. But that doesn't mean you won't contract a sexually transmitted disease if your partner was infected or you won't get pregnant if the "seed" was sown.

When we sow to the flesh, we reap the consequences. The consequences teach us to abhor sin and to fear God. King David understood all of this. There is no record of his ever being bitter toward God. He bore his punishment as a man of God should, and from that came some of the most encouraging and inspiring words of hope that mankind would ever possess, the psalms. Some were written after David's sin with Bathsheba. One of them was Psalm 51.

The second consequence of adultery can be divorce. Many marriages scarred by unfaithfulness do end in divorce. While God offers forgiveness, He hates divorce, which violates the physical oneness of husband and wife. It is contrary to His plan for marriage. Jesus taught that people should not view divorce as a morally acceptable option (see Matt. 19).

The third consequence is damage to our children. Adultery frequently causes a child to stumble. It gives our children the wrong example, a distorted picture of the sanctity of marriage. Malachi 2:15 says if you are seeking godly offspring, you don't divorce your mate and you don't cover your garment with wrong. God warns us that the sins of the fathers are passed on to the next generation (Ex. 34:7). It becomes a sickening cycle: immorality to divorce, divorce to immorality, and so on.

Fourth, adultery and a consequent divorce scars and may destroy the family unit and put the children at risk. Even in the best situations, remarriage frequently brings conflict into a blended family. A child's discipline may become a topic for disagreement: "Whose child is this anyway?" "My loyalty is to my child!" Remarriage also can put a child at risk of physical and sexual abuse. My files are filled with stories of lives scarred by abuse.

Can you see what happens? Immorality breaks a husband and wife's oneness which in turn destroys the child's security and protection. I cannot tell you how many calls Jan Silvious and I answered on this very issue during five years of a live call-in program—not to mention the letters we received of the children who were unbelievably traumatized.

Fifth, adultery truly hurts God. Remember this fact when you are tempted to meet your lover for a stolen hour in bed—a bed in which you have no right to be!

Look at Ezekiel 6:9, where God spoke to Israel, His wife by covenant. Listen as He recounted her adultery. As you read the verse, mark the references to adultery and harlotry. Draw a heart over the word *heart*.

"Then those of you who escape will remember Me among the nations to which they will be carried captive, how I have been hurt by their adulterous hearts which turned away from Me, and by their eyes which played the harlot after their idols; and they will loathe themselves in their own sight for the evils which they have committed, for all their abominations."

Rest assured, the immoral, those who have lived in adultery, will loathe themselves. What once seemed sweet will become the gall of bitterness. Grieved beyond measure, they will stand face-to-face before God—the One whose heart they grieved. Wives whose husbands have been unfaithful know something of the pain. Hear the *pathos* of God's cry when He said to Israel, "You adulteress wife, who takes strangers instead of her husband!" (Ezek. 16:32).

What had the adulteress wife done to so grieve her husband? God tells us in Ezekiel 16, and in the telling there is much for us to learn. Watch the path of her seduction.

Underline every "you" and "your" and put a red *H* over every reference to harlot and harlotry. Mark the word *heart* with a heart.

EZEKIEL 16:15-17,20-21,25-26,28-30
15 But you trusted in your beauty and played the harlot because of your fame, and you poured out your harlotries on every passer-by who might be willing.
16 You took some of your clothes, made for yourself high places of various colors and played the harlot on them, which should never come about nor happen.
17 You also took your beautiful jewels made of My gold and of My silver, which I had given you, and made for yourself male images that you might play the harlot with them.
. . . .
20 Moreover, you took your sons and daughters whom you had borne to Me and sacrificed them to idols to be devoured. Were your harlotries so small a matter?
21 You slaughtered My children, and offered them up to idols by causing them to pass through the fire.
. . . .
25 You built yourself a high place at the top of every street and made your beauty abominable, and you spread your legs to every passer-by to multiply your harlotry.
26 You also played the harlot with the Egyptians, your lustful neighbors, and multiplied your harlotry to make Me angry.

²⁸ Moreover, you played the harlot with the Assyrians because you were not satisfied; you played the harlot with them and still were not satisfied.

²⁹ You also multiplied your harlotry with the land of merchants, Chaldea, yet even with this you were not satisfied.

³⁰ "How languishing is your heart," declares the Lord God, "while you do all these things, the actions of a bold-faced harlot."

What did you learn from marking the references to you? List what God's "wife" had done.

Note the progression—it starts with *her beauty*—her focus is the external. Not that we shouldn't be attractive to our husbands; they love it! However, she is preoccupied with how she looks and how she dresses. What effort it takes to achieve the image she wants! Then it becomes an image—what she worships, gives herself to, bows down before; worshiping, as Romans 1 says, the creature rather than the Creator. She is her preoccupation. She becomes her own idol! And eventually she sacrifices her children on the altar of her lust. No wonder God's heart is grieved.

Sixth and finally for our study, adultery—or immorality in any form—gives cause for the enemies of God to blaspheme His name! Nathan told King David as much in 2 Samuel 12:14. The world holds Christians to a higher standard and finds great delight in our fall. It makes us just like them! And they have their excuse to do the same, or so they think!

Well, there it is, fellow female. Don't treat this lesson lightly— we must listen, hear, and be warned. We must think on these things. Consider them. Talk to God about them. Never forget that God is not a respecter of persons: "Adulterers and fornicators God will judge." May the fear, respect, and trust of Him be in our hearts.

IT'S A WAR
OUT THERE

In our final day of study on the seductress and how not to be one, we must understand the warfare men endure and how we, as women, can contribute to it if we are not careful. We read in Proverbs 7 about the "strange woman" and how she dressed, how she came "to meet him dressed as a harlot." Now, how do you think a harlot dresses?

Look around you! You can't miss it! Our clothes look as if fabric is rationed. The blouse doesn't cover the waistline, the pants hug the hips, and more often than not a rolling hill of fat lies in between. Jeans are so sparsely cut that they gather, grab, tuck, and pinch every square inch of flesh. Then they're zipped with great effort. Skirts have so little material that one can't bend over, sit down, or slide out of a car without trying to pull it down—unless of course you don't care if someone peeks.

Strike the pose. There they are in bathing suits held together by strings, the bottoms sassily held up by a thumb, the tops straining to cover the curves of newly-enhanced breasts. And sad to say, there are the tweens who either dress like their mothers or wear their mothers' hand-me-downs until they are able to buy clothes like their friends wear.

I wonder if we really understand the damage we do when we dress this way? Think of the torment we create in the minds of men.

SEX IS ON HIS BRAIN

No! Don't say it! They are not "just dirty old men." They're men and men of all ages are turned on by sight! That is how God made them. Sex is on their brains. What they see can instantly turn to sex on the mind. Let me show you in the Word.

> Let's look at Jesus' teaching a crowd in Matthew 15.
> Read it—aloud of course! Then we will mark it.

MATTHEW 15:10-11,15-20

¹⁰ After Jesus called the crowd to Him, He said to them, "Hear and understand.

¹¹ "It is not what enters into the mouth that defiles the man, but what proceeds out of the mouth, this defiles the man."

. . . .

¹⁵ Peter said to Him, "Explain the parable to us."

¹⁶ Jesus said, "Are you still lacking in understanding also?

¹⁷ "Do you not understand that everything that goes into the mouth passes into the stomach, and is eliminated?

¹⁸ "But the things that proceed out of the mouth come from the heart, and those defile the man.

¹⁹ "For out of the heart come evil thoughts, murders, adulteries, fornications, thefts, false witness, slanders.

²⁰ "These are the things which defile the man; but to eat with unwashed hands does not defile the man."

OK, now read it again and mark the references to the heart. Color-code or mark the word *defile*.

Did you see the list in verse 19? (You may want to number lists.) Let's focus on what God is teaching in this passage by asking some questions.

What defiles a man?

Where does it come from?

What are the things that come from the heart?

How many of those things have to do with a person's sexuality? Underline them in the passage.

Have you wondered why you find adulteries and fornications in the same list? Let's review. Generally in the Bible, *adultery* refers to an act of unfaithfulness in marriage that occurs when one of the marriage partners voluntarily engages in sexual intercourse with a person other than the marriage partner. *Fornication* is a broader term that encompasses various types of sexual immorality.

Remember what you observed. These are things that come from the heart. The *kardía* is used figuratively in the New Testament as "the seat of the desires, feelings, affections, passions, impulses, i.e., the heart or mind."[3] When you read *heart*, think *mind*! The most powerful sex organ is the mind! The mind is stimulated primarily by what it sees. Are you beginning to get the picture, dear one? The way you dress can turn on a man!

Let me share some of Fred Stoeker's story. The co-author of *Every Man's Battle* is a man like many whom you pass day after day.

> "My eyes ... were ravenous heat-seekers searching the horizon, locking on any target with sensual heat. Young mothers leaning over in shorts to pull children out of car seat. Soloists with silky shirts. Summer dresses with décolletage. My mind, too, ran wherever it willed. This had begun in my childhood, when I found *Playboy* magazines under Dad's bed. He also subscribed to *From Sex to Sexty*, a publication filled with jokes and comic strips with sexual themes. When Dad divorced Mom and moved to his 'bachelor's pad,' he hung a giant velvet nude in his living room, overlooking us as we played cards on my Sunday afternoon visits. ... All this sexual stuff churned deep inside of me, destroying a purity that wouldn't return for many years."[4]

Listen to Jesus in His heart-searching Sermon on the Mount. Read Matthew 5:27-30 and mark every reference to adultery. You'll also want to mark the word *heart*.

MATTHEW 5: 27-30

27 "You have heard that it was said, 'YOU SHALL NOT COMMIT ADULTERY';

28 but I say to you that everyone who looks at a woman with lust for her has already committed adultery with her in his heart.

29 "If your right eye makes you stumble, tear it out and throw it from you; for it is better for you to lose one of the parts of your body, than for your whole body to be thrown into hell.

30 "If your right hand makes you stumble, cut it off and throw it from you; for it is better for you to lose one of the parts of your body, than for your whole body to go into hell."

Now as you observed the text, did you notice the reference to the eyes, to looking? Why don't you draw eyeballs like this over those references? It will give you a great visual.

Look at the words you marked. What did you learn?

ADULTERY   HEART   EYEBALLS

What is Jesus' point?

Finally, remembering that the best interpreter of Scripture
is Scripture, what did you learn about the importance of
what a man sees?

Do you better understand the lure of pornography?
Explain your answer.

Although we will not deal extensively with pornography in this study,
The Truth About Sex covers what the Bible has to say on the subject for men
and women. I strongly recommend that you study the book with your
daughter(s) and that your husband take your son(s) through it. Such a
study between parents and their children is desperately needed.

Now, precious lady, do you think God will hold you responsible for the way you dress? Why? (It's always good to know why!)

What message are you sending, consciously or unconsciously, by the way you dress?

THE GATEWAY TO SIN

One last Old Testament Scripture and we finish for the week.

Read Job 31:1-4. Color-code every reference to God or put a triangle over every reference to Him: for example, *Almighty, He.* Draw eyeballs over any reference to the eyes or to the action of looking.

JOB 31:1-4

1 "I have made a covenant with my eyes;
   How then could I gaze at a virgin?
2 "And what is the portion of God from above
   Or the heritage of the Almighty from on high?
3 "Is it not calamity to the unjust
   And disaster to those who work iniquity?
4 "Does He not see my ways
   And number all my steps?"

What do you learn from marking the references to God?

What happens to those who are unjust, to those who sin
or work iniquity?

What did you learn from the eyeballs?

Now let's look at Job 31:9-12. Once again, mark
any reference to the heart.

JOB 31:9-12

⁹ "If my heart has been enticed by a woman,
    Or I have lurked at my neighbor's doorway,
¹⁰ May my wife grind for another,
    And let others kneel down over her.
¹¹ "For that would be a lustful crime;
    Moreover, it would be an iniquity punishable by judges.
¹² "For it would be fire that consumes to Abaddon,
    And would uproot all my increase.

**With what subject was Job dealing? What was he saying—
and how does it connect with what you have studied today?**

As you look at Job, you see the responsibility of the man to turn away from anything that might tempt him. He knew that the gateway to adultery is the eyes—the heart, the mind—and so he made a covenant, or a solemn binding agreement with his eyes (Job 31:1). He would not look on a woman.

There you have it—in the Old Testament and in the New Testament. Adultery, sexual immorality, begins with the eyes and in the mind. Stop it there—or you are guilty before God, and a holy God will have to punish your sin.

Now can you better appreciate the little Christian chorus "O Be Careful, Little Eyes"? Should not this be our song so we do not play the role of a seductress?

> Be careful little maid how you dress,
> Be careful little maid what you show,
> For the Father up above is looking down in love
> Be careful little maid how you dress.

I am so proud of you, faithful one. Learn this song, and sing it when you stand in front of that mirror. Bend down—what's on display for the person in front of you? Sit down—are you covered? If his eyes catch your ankles, how far up can they go and see flesh? Do you have a slit in your skirt? What do people see when you cross your legs? When you bend over, what's the rear view? Where would it take his mind?

Now remember, you're not your own. You've been bought with a price, so glorify God by the way you dress His temple. And when it comes to the way your daughter dresses—remember, you are the parent and you will give an account to God. Your daughter needs a parent, not another girlfriend. Parent her.

Finally, I'll leave you with one last suggestion: Talk to God about checking out your closet this week. If you wouldn't wear it in public with Jesus, it has to go—unless, of course, it's for your husband in the privacy of your bedroom. A change in my wardrobe was one of the first things that happened when I became a child of God! Ask Jesus to help you with your decisions.

Viewer Guide
SESSION 5

THE SEDUCTRESS (AND HOW NOT TO BE ONE)

It is the cross and the _____ _____ that enables us to live a life of purity.

_____ yourself with Jesus Christ.

I'm talking about being a _____ of Jesus Christ.

It's a _____ _____ with no absolutes.

THE WAY LOVE *Should Be*

We've dealt with so much in our study together—with how sin has tainted God's design, with how sex has become dirty, distorted, and destructive to many people. Perhaps you feel that nothing beautiful could come from your actions or mistakes. Remember how we first began by talking about God's original plan for sex to serve as a picture of Christ's divine love for His bride? Tragically, we've seen that humans have twisted and perverted this metaphor until it's barely recognizable.

Oh, how I wish I could say this to you in person: There is *still* hope no matter how far you've deviated either unintentionally or willfully from what is right. You can recover; your loved ones can recover. Our society could recover! Can you imagine how such a movement of purity might transform our world today!

THIS WEEK, THROUGH YOUR
HOME STUDY, YOU WILL:

grow in your love for studying God's Word

figuratively "return to the garden" as you
realize again how special is God's gift of sex

recognize the importance to your marriage
of meeting your husband's sexual needs and
make appropriate commitments

be reminded of ways to guard your heart
from cultural temptations

(Where needed) *allow* God to change you as
you seek His forgiveness and/or place yourself
in the position to minister to other women

A GLIMPSE INTO PURE INTIMACY

Today as we look at courtship and marriage the way each should be— a man and a woman enraptured only with one another and not ashamed to let it be known—let's begin with this illustration.

> We were going over a proposal and couldn't make sense of the dollar figures.
>
> As I sat at the conference table, staring at the numbers, trying to figure it all out, I found myself suddenly bathed in the luscious fragrance of perfume. Wondering where it came from and why I hadn't smelled it before, I looked up from the papers spread before me into the softness of breasts cradled in lace. My associate was bending over the table, trying to explain to me where the mistake was!
>
> It was over. From that moment on, I couldn't think of any other problem than how I was going to get home and get the kids in bed early so I could have sex with my wife.[1]

This, beloved, is the way it should be—a one-woman man! His wife was on his mind—not the woman who was bending over him. His wife's breasts, not those of a stranger, are to satisfy a man (see Prov. 5).

What can we learn in this final week that will help our husbands keep *us* on their minds? And what if we have failed to meet God's standard in the areas we have studied over the past four weeks? Well, dear one, we will cover that as well so that you will finish this course with the knowledge that all is well between you and your Father God and that it is going to get even better with your husband. What if you are still single?

Is there anything for you? Of course, there is; if you don't have an earthly bridegroom, you have a heavenly one and a wedding to come.

THE BEAUTY OF SEX IN MARRIAGE

God has included an amazing book in His holy Book. Song of Solomon gives us a glimpse into the intimacy God intended for us when He created us male and female and brought the woman to the man. It tells the love story of King Solomon and his Shulammite bride.

Here is a love to be rejoiced in, extolled, for the Shulammite (Song of Sol. 6:13) has found one whom her soul loves. The resulting "Song of Songs"—the best of songs (1:1)—is primarily a dialogue between the bride and the bridegroom, with choruses interjected by "daughters of Jerusalem" (v. 5). This dialogue provides insights that will keep us on our husbands' minds. If you study the Songs inductively, you will want to carefully mark the book to know who is speaking and when.

In this study our focus is only on the portions pertinent to the beauty of sex in marriage. In the first two chapters we glimpse their courtship; then in 3:6–5:2 we join the wedding party and read of the consummation of their marriage. From there to the end of Song of Solomon we see "love tried and triumphant."

> **As you come to the word *love* anywhere in the text, mark it throughout these days of study. Also underline the word *beloved* as you come across it.**

> **At one time or another, the overwhelming majority of women dream of marriage. We dream of love, kisses, and _____. You fill in the blank.**

"May he kiss me with the kisses of his mouth!" (Song of Sol. 1:2). She wanted to be kissed! How well I remember that longing. Once I experienced the wonder of my lips touching those of my husband, it was hard for me to think of anything else. And my kisses were special to him!

Solomon and his beautiful woman felt the same way about each other. Quite possibly she had never kissed another man. Listen to their conversation. Follow their words closely; notice how they expressed their desires and their appreciation of each other.

SONG OF SOLOMON 1:9-11

9 "To me, my darling, you are like
   My mare among the chariots of Pharaoh.
10 "Your cheeks are lovely with ornaments,
   Your neck with strings of beads.
11 "We will make for you ornaments of gold
   With beads of silver."

This is Middle Eastern talk from more than two thousand years ago. In those times men were as attached to their horses as men today are to their cars. They decorated their steeds with ornaments that jingled, jangled, and flashed in the sun. You might compare it to American cars of the 50s and 60s—revved-up, painted with lightning streaks, and decorated with fuzzy dice dangling from the rear-view mirror. Even today men equip their cars with all sorts of tires, hubcaps, and electronic gadgets that cause other guys to say, "Whoa man! You've got it all!"

Well, Solomon, the groom, had it all—an outstanding horse and an outstanding woman! His mare showed up the mares of Pharaoh and his darling was "the most beautiful of women."

And what about this young maid standing at the well where he watered his flocks? Listen to her describe the man who had captured her heart:

SONG OF SOLOMON 1:13-14

13 "My beloved is to me a pouch of myrrh
   Which lies all night between my breasts.
14 "My beloved is to me a cluster of henna blossoms
   In the vineyards of Engedi."

Solomon sweetened her life; the thought of him was nothing but pleasant. He brought a fragrance into her life, like that of myrrh and henna.

Oh, how people love to be around others who make them feel good about themselves! How does your husband sweeten *your* life?

And what did he think of his wife? Watch how he responded: "How beautiful you are, my darling, how beautiful you are! Your eyes are like doves" (Song of Sol. 1:15). Solomon loved her eyes, describing them as dove's eyes. He loved hearing what her eyes see. Did you know that doves' eyes focus only on one thing? Let your husband know that you have dove's eyes when it comes to him. Don't compare him with others, dear one, unless he comes out on top!

Did you notice that before Solomon talked to the Shulammite maiden about her body, he talked to her about her eyes? Today in our sex-obsessed society a woman often evaluates herself based on the size of her breasts, the tightness of her abs, or the flatness of her stomach. Sallie Foley, a sex therapist and one author of *Sex Matters for Women*, has observed, "Generation X women are having dramatic problems being satisfied with the body they bring into the bedroom. Gen X women have internalized this sense of the body perfect, and that is an impossible ideal. They think if they have a perfect body, they will have better sex, and that shows a profound misunderstanding about sexuality. It's simply not true that women who have infomercial bodies are having better sex."[2]

IN HIGHEST ESTEEM

The Song of Solomon is a classic because it's not about the body, although the bride and bridegroom greatly appreciated one another's bodies. Rather, it is about love as God intended it—for pleasure, but not in a tawdry way. In this book love is not smeared on the streets or in the locker rooms; its purity and sacredness remain untainted by trash talk. And there is no comparison.

This woman was appreciated for who she was, as she was. She didn't feel cheap, like a sex toy or a porn star. She felt valued. How important feeling valued is to a beautiful sexual relationship!

In some marriages the wife feels devalued, often for reasons that need to be corrected and dealt with. If you want your physical relationship to soar, hold your beloved in the highest of esteem. Love begets love, and gracious words produce more gracious words: "How handsome you are, my beloved, And so pleasant!" (Song of Sol. 1:16).

Isn't this what we want and need to hear—that we are special in the eyes of our beloved, that we ourselves are beloved? Twenty-seven times she referred to Solomon as beloved. Many hearts long to be called *beloved!* Women tell me over and over again how much it means to them for me to address them with that term. "No one ever called me that before." Men need to know they're beloved too, special to someone. *Beloved* is used throughout the epistles as men of God wrote to the people of God. Do you have a term of endearment that lets your husband know how special he is to you?

As we continue reading in Song of Solomon 2, listen as this bride-to-be reveled in her uniqueness. Observe as she delighted in how special they were to each other. What a difference a healthy self-image makes in a marriage!

Mark the words *I* and *me* in one color for the woman and in a different color for the man.

The woman was speaking:
"I am the rose of Sharon, the lily of the valleys" (v. 1).

He agreed and responded:
"Like a lily among the thorns, so is my darling among the maidens" (v. 2).

She had chosen him! He had won the prize! What an ego builder to a man, to think that the woman he is about to marry is incredibly special— and what a wonder this awareness was to his bride. This is the kind of a man a woman wants to cover, sustain, and hold her.

SONG OF SOLOMON 2:3-6

³ "Like an apple tree among the trees of the forest,
   So is my beloved among the young men.
   In his shade I took great delight and sat down,
   And his fruit was sweet to my taste.
⁴ He has brought me to his banquet hall,
   And his banner over me is love.
⁵ Sustain me with raisin cakes,
   Refresh me with apples,
   Because I am lovesick.
⁶ Let his left hand be under my head
   And his right hand embrace me."

Do you hear the conversation, the admiration as she leaned on him verbally, expressing her delight in his provision? Yet in all their verbally expressed passion for one another, they were aware that they must be cautious. The Shulammite and her husband-to-be knew what desires waged war in their flesh. Love was not to be awakened until it was time. Listen to his caution: "Daughters of Jerusalem, I charge you by the gazelles and by the does of the field: Do not arouse or awaken love until it so desires" (v. 7, NIV).

Variations of this phrase are repeated both in Song of Solomon 3:5 and 8:4. Solomon urged the daughters of Jerusalem to remain pure, to not awaken love when it could not be fulfilled. He admonished them—and us—to be vigilant against any compromise that would taint the relationship with the opposite sex. Love is to be expressed sexually in only one place and that is in the marriage bed.

GUARDING YOUR HEART

In the same chapter note a similar warning in the verse concerning what the foxes want to do to the vineyard: "Catch the foxes for us, the little foxes that are ruining the vineyards, while our vineyards are in blossom" (v. 15). Watch out for the foxes that want to steal your fruit!

How I wish I'd heard and heeded this advice in my youth! I wish I'd been warned about the little things that would steal the beauty of innocence. It's hard for me to believe that I became an immoral woman. Sensuality was in my mind from childhood because of the things I saw and imagined, but purity was my desire. It would have been so wonderful to have known only one man all my life, to have realized what I longed for in a marriage, what I saved myself for. Being the perfectionist I am, it is a grief I battle, especially when I write books on sexuality or marriage. I have to continually bring my grief and regret in submission to all I know from the Scriptures: "Forgetting what lies behind [and what I can never change] ... I press on toward the goal for the prize of the upward call of God in Christ Jesus" (Phil. 3:13-14).

The Shulammite would never have to deal with such things, and I pray you won't either. However, if you do, I can tell you there's victory if you will do what God tells you to do.

If you want to know the pure beauty of being one flesh with your husband, do everything you can to protect your mind and your eyes; guard yourself from sexual experiences that aren't according to God's plan. When you wait, when you guard your mind, when you don't permit your eyes to watch others in immoral acts—then you come to the marriage bed with no expectations, no comparisons. You have known no one else, so you and your husband can explore and discover together. If you catch the foxes before they eat your innocence, you will have the high and unique privilege of initiating each other into the wonder of love. And while it may take some time to know how to please one another, it will be beautiful because it is untainted by the world.

THE WEDDING DAY

In chapter 3 we come to the marriage as Solomon and his companions—60 mighty men—go to get his bride. It is the day of their wedding. "Go forth, O daughters of Zion, and gaze on King Solomon with the crown with which his mother has crowned him on the day of his wedding, and on the day of his gladness of heart" (Song of Sol. 3:11).

No shame. No guilt. No child in the womb. A white dress and purity. There is gladness of heart, for at long last they will know each other in the fullness of the word.

The day is marked forever in their minds and hearts, a day set apart and awaited. This is the day she will give her bridegroom the gift she can give only once, and he will know he is the first—and the last. This is the day they will become one flesh in the literal sense of the word.

Now he talked to her of love and of the beauty of her body in words that seem strange to us in our culture and times, but they were beautiful to her and not smut, filth, or Internet chat-room talk with someone she'd never seen. His words extolled who she was, what he knew of her. She would cherish these erotic but pure words for a lifetime. He chose these words to awaken love, for now it was in God's time.

The "Song of Songs" is devoted to the beauty of an undefiled marriage bed. Written and preserved for a thousand generations, its timeless truths never change. This is God's textbook for those who would listen to His precepts and keep them, those who would experience the beauty of becoming one flesh.

Now, beloved, if you are single, reflect on what you want on your wedding day. What kind of a woman do you want your bridegroom to have? What kind of a bridegroom do you want? Write some thoughts here or on a separate piece of paper, as a special reminder for when that day comes.

If what you wish for is not possible because of your past, be patient as we will deal with that circumstance near the end of this week. You can have a new beginning—as good as God can make it. And remember, He is the Redeemer.

If you are married, you cannot change your wedding night, but you can take the truths we've seen and apply them. So stop and review what you're read and then list some things you want to do or remember so that your marriage is the best you can make it—whether or not your husband cooperates.

And what is your prayer? Write it here.

DAY TWO

BEHIND CLOSED
DOORS

Do you realize that Song of Solomon is the only time God ever takes us behind closed doors into a bridal chamber? Listen carefully to what Solomon said in chapter 4 to his darling bride as he consummated their covenant of marriage.

Color-code every reference to the wife in chapter 4. (Remember, much of this is Middle Eastern language over 2,000 years ago!) Underline the various references to her body that Solomon mentioned and notice what he said.

SONG OF SOLOMON 4:1-15

[1] "How beautiful you are, my darling,
How beautiful you are!
Your eyes are like doves behind your veil;
Your hair is like a flock of goats
That have descended from Mount Gilead.

[2] Your teeth are like a flock of newly shorn ewes
Which have come up from their washing,
All of which bear twins,
And not one among them has lost her young.

[3] Your lips are like a scarlet thread,
And your mouth is lovely.
Your temples are like a slice of a pomegranate
Behind your veil.

[4] Your neck is like the tower of David,
Built with rows of stones
On which are hung a thousand shields,
All the round shields of the mighty men.

[5] Your two breasts are like two fawns,
Twins of a gazelle,
Which feed among the lilies.

[6] Until the cool of the day
When the shadows flee away,
I will go my way to the mountain of myrrh
And to the hill of frankincense.

[7] You are altogether beautiful, my darling,
And there is no blemish in you.

[8] Come with me from Lebanon, my bride,
May you come with me from Lebanon.
Journey down from the summit of Amana,
From the summit of Senir and Hermon,
From the dens of lions,
From the mountains of leopards.

⁹ You have made my heart beat faster, my sister, my bride;
  You have made my heart beat faster with a single glance
      of your eyes,
  With a single strand of your necklace.
¹⁰ How beautiful is your love, my sister, my bride!
  How much better is your love than wine,
  And the fragrance of your oils
  Than all kinds of spices!
¹¹ Your lips, my bride, drip honey;
  Honey and milk are under your tongue,
  And the fragrance of your garments is like
      the fragrance of Lebanon.
¹² A garden locked is my sister, my bride,
  A rock garden locked, a spring sealed up.
¹³ Your shoots are an orchard of pomegranates
  With choice fruits, henna with nard plants,
¹⁴ Nard and saffron, calamus and cinnamon,
  With all the trees of frankincense,
  Myrrh and aloes, along with all the finest spices.
¹⁵ You are a garden spring,
  A well of fresh water,
  And streams flowing from Lebanon."

**Did he make any comparisons with other women?
Any put-downs?**

This is the beauty of sex as God intended it to be. Did you grasp all he
was saying? Read these verses again and ponder the bridegroom's words.

This time mark:
- the word *garden* with a color or a symbol
- the phrase *with me* in another distinctive way

And what is the garden, bearing luscious fruits, locked until now? What is this spring of fresh water that has been sealed (vv. 12-15)?

And what was her response to her beloved? Watch how she responded.

SONG OF SOLOMON 4:16
"Awake, O north wind,
And come, wind of the south;
Make my garden breathe out fragrance,
Let its spices be wafted abroad.
May my beloved come into his garden
And eat its choice fruits!"

As a woman, why do you think the Shulammite responded the way she did?

Her garden that had been locked up was the purity of virginity, a holy innocence to be discovered and delighted in. And she was ready for it to be unlocked. She had not been rushed. He had considered her needs. He had not just taken her; he had admired her, and now she longed for him. "May my beloved come into *his* garden."

She was his. His alone. Just as God intended.

SACRED LOVE

When sex is as God intended, it is more than passion; it is beautiful, comfortable. "Naked and not ashamed." There's no need to put on, to cover up, or to perform. It is a far cry from what it is portrayed on many movie, television, and Internet screens; these are man's version—his picture of raw, animal passion.

What we see in the Song of Solomon is sacred love. This is a love that frees one another from performance, from keeping up with the bodies, passion, or the panting of others. This is for the two of you alone. Free from the critics and the analysts. This is where you discover and please each other—and if you are not being satisfied, sacred love means helping one another, being patient and understanding. This is where you are secure in one another's love and commitment regardless of what happens or doesn't happen on any particular night.

A single friend told me of another friend who wearied of waiting for sex until marriage. When no one who suited her proposed marriage, she decided to experience sex on her next business trip. The whole thing was carefully calculated. She scanned the crowd, picked out a single man, and went to bed with him. That night she surrendered her virginity to a man who meant nothing to her, a man she didn't even know.

When she got home, she called my friend to tell her about the weekend. Her words of pathos stuck in my friend's memory: "Is this what poets write about? Is this the subject of love songs, the themes of great movies?"

Her first sexual experience was disappointing, a disheartening letdown. Why? I believe it's because the encounter didn't take place in God's intended setting of marriage, a commitment for life that promises monogamy until death. "I have come into my garden, my sister, my bride; I have gathered my myrrh along with my balsam. I have eaten my honeycomb and my honey; I have drunk my wine and my milk" (5:1).

The wife satisfied her bridegroom. This is how it should be. Remember the man at the beginning of our study this week, the man who smelled the sweet fragrance of another woman, who saw her breasts and wanted his wife?[1]

What could you do, precious lady, to strengthen your relationship with your husband?

Do you pray for your husband? Why don't you bring today's study to a close by writing out your prayer for him and for yourself?

If you are single and think God has a husband for you, why don't you write out a prayer for him right now? God knows who he is, where he is, and when he'll arrive.

DELIGHTING IN
ONENESS

My friend turned to me as she walked out the door. "My kids (they're in their 20's) would never buy this book. They would laugh at it. It is so contrary to what they believe, where they live."

"I know," I interrupted, "and it breaks my heart. A lot of people will never buy its content. But I had to write it so at least people—teens and adults—would know what God says, what can be theirs if they will only listen to Him and believe what He says."

My friend had just finished reading the manuscript of *The Truth About Sex* and was getting ready to drive back to Atlanta. She hesitated and then asked, "Do you really believe people think sex is beautiful? Most of the people I know don't."

In her words I heard the emptiness of a thousand generations who wished sex had been beautiful. They didn't want to hear that it could have been because they never found it to be so.

Sex as God intended it is beautiful—but not always passionate, exciting, or even personally satisfying. But that does not take away its beauty. If you will understand its necessity for a healthy, strong marriage and will honor what God says, sex will take on a beauty all its own.

Let's return to Song of Solomon. The wedding is scarcely over and the bride has made a foolish mistake.

Read the following verses and color-code the references to our woman and her husband so you can keep them straight. The woman was speaking.

SONG OF SOLOMON 5:2-6
2 "I was asleep, but my heart was awake.
  A voice! My beloved was knocking:

'Open to me, my sister, my darling,
My dove, my perfect one!
For my head is drenched with dew,
My locks with the damp of the night.'
³ I have taken off my dress,
How can I put it on again?
I have washed my feet,
How can I dirty them again?
⁴ My beloved extended his hand through the opening,
And my feelings were aroused for him.
⁵ I arose to open to my beloved;
And my hands dripped with myrrh,
And my fingers with liquid myrrh,
On the handles of the bolt.
⁶ I opened to my beloved,
But my beloved had turned away and had gone!
My heart went out to him as he spoke.
I searched for him but I did not find him;
I called him but he did not answer me."

Sometimes sex is a bother. You're too tired, busy, preoccupied, engrossed or it's late, you have a headache, or you just don't feel like it . . . whatever! We can come up with 101 reasons not to, forgetting that love involves sacrifice and includes meeting your mate's needs when you don't want to do so. Maybe it's not convenient, it's uncomfortable, it's not on your time-table; but you should do it anyway for the sake of love, not passion.

"But it's *my* body," you groan. "And I don't feel like it! I don't want it. Why can't I say no and have a clear conscience?"

In 1 Corinthians 7 God has given us His general rule of thumb for when married couples should have sex. Read it and color every reference to the wife and to the husband, just as you did when marking Song of Solomon.

I CORINTHIANS 7:2-5

² But because of immoralities, each man is to have his own
   wife, and each woman is to have her own husband.
³ The husband must fulfill his duty to his wife, and likewise
   also the wife to her husband.
⁴ The wife does not have authority over her own body, but
   the husband does; and likewise also the husband does not
   have authority over his own body, but the wife does.
⁵ Stop depriving one another, except by agreement for a time,
   so that you may devote yourselves to prayer, and come
   together again so that Satan will not tempt you because
   of your lack of self-control.

List under each column what you learn from these verses:

THE HUSBAND   THE WIFE

What would you say the "when" is for sex?

To me, the answer seems to be *when needed, when sex is asked for.* Men usually
need intercourse more often than their wives. As we have seen, it's a
matter of the eyes for men—and in a culture permeated with sex, they
are bombarded with visual images that trigger the switch in their brains.
For women it is a matter of touch, and even then, we want the circumstances to be just right.

IN LOVE, SERVE YOUR HUSBAND

Yet in verse 4 we learn that when we marry, each of us surrenders the authority of our body to our spouse. We've given up our right to say no. Of course, there needs to be consideration and understanding on the part of whoever's doing the asking—which most often will be the man. However, I don't think either person will want to deprive the other when we remember that love serves another and endures all things! It's tough to be burning with desire and not be able to legitimately satisfy it with your husband. It's frustrating.

One of our Precept study leaders told me how God taught her—in a very scary and graphic way—the importance of meeting her husband's sexual needs. (I've edited to keep their privacy.)

> I fell deeply into my role as a mother. God had given me three beautiful children, and they became the center of my world. Those early days were so exhausting. By the time Mike would get home from work, I would be so tired. I knew he was drawing away some and seemed quiet, but I was too tired to worry. I'd go to bed early, and he would stay up later working upstairs on the computer.
>
> He knew I was tired, and he didn't want to push me for attention. As the days went on, he began to feel I no longer liked him. He began to be drawn to pornography, and I was not meeting his sexual desires. He decided not to have an affair, since all he really wanted was sexual attention and he knew an affair was wrong.
>
> He became interested in the Internet sites. One night he decided to send out a homosexual request so he could meet someone on his next business trip. He still loved me; he just wanted the attention, so this seemed reasonable to him and I'd never know.
>
> So he typed in the request and as he does, he copied it into the buffer space with a CTRL-C. The next day I was editing something on the computer and by

accident hit the CTRL-V, which copied what he put into the buffer into my document. (Have you got chill bumps yet?) So here in my documents was "MWM, 5-11, seeks homosexual experience." It took me a minute. I thought it was a computer virus, but then it hit home what this really was. I was cut to the core. I couldn't believe this of him. I called him at work to come home early, and we began to talk.

As truly awful as these days were, we both knew we had been touched by God. By these unusual circumstances we knew God had given us a huge wake-up call. He had intervened at just the moment when an awful mistake could have done serious damage. I don't deny we still had big problems, but they could have been so much worse if other people had become involved.

My friend learned a great lesson about the importance of meeting her husband's sexual needs and making him feel like the most important person in her life, next to Jesus. And what's the story several years later?

Our marriage is better and stronger than ever before. We are so happy. I know that all those old-fashioned marriage ideas my mom used to tell me are so important. I just wish she had told me why and pointed me to the Word of God for biblical reasons. We must love our husbands and make them feel loved and special.

To be honest, we're scared to mess up; we are afraid of what God might do this time. But ours is more than a good marriage; through our experience and through Precept, we are stronger Christians. Our lives have been changed, and we are living for Him now.

So what do you do when your husband won't—or can't—meet your sexual needs? The first thing you need to do is find out why. It might be as simple as a loss of desire because of too little sleep. There may be other physical reasons—or it may be emotional, a lack of self-worth. It could be a number of reasons that we won't pursue, but you need to find out because it is good for your relationship as well as for your body for a couple to have sex.

However, what do you do if it comes to the place where one partner cannot or will not fulfill his or her duty? Then, beloved, you have to live with it the same way a single person has to live without sex. God's grace is sufficient; it has to be because there is no other legitimate way to satisfy your desire. So ask Him for His power in your weakness and move on, avoiding those things that arouse and awaken your desires—guarding your heart, keeping your thoughts under His control. Remember sex in marriage is important, but it is only one aspect of the relationship.

I've kept a note scribbled on the back of an advertisement for an occasion like this because it touched my heart and made me very proud of my sister in Christ. She writes, "I'm not sure you remember the letter I wrote to you about two years ago. It was about the lack of intimacy in my relationship with my husband. Well, it's been six years now, in April, and it's still lacking. But I am at peace with this because I do feel the love he has for me, regardless of the sexual part of it. Thanks for the wonderful study material. It's has helped me greatly!"

I left the last two sentences in because I think they explain where her strength and perspective come from—studying God's Word inductively, discovering truth for herself so that she knows that she knows. Beloved, you'll find that His Word can get you through any situation.

And what sustains the beauty of sex? Valuing it. Giving sex the time and attention it needs. In chapter 5, when the Shulammite didn't meet her husband's needs, it seemed she was too tired to get out of bed and put on something and come to the door. She had washed her feet and would have to wash them again. It was wearying. Even when she saw him trying to reach the bolt through the window and open the door himself, she didn't move until it was too late.

Our schedules are so jammed that we are too exhausted for sex—and it is sex that nurtures a marriage. Good sex takes time if both partners are to be satisfied. Therefore, whether or not you work outside the home, make sure you don't neglect your sexual relationship.

YEARNING TO BE WITH HIM

The Shulammite soon recognized her mistake in not rousing herself for her husband. She yearned to be with him with the same longing she felt before their wedding. "I sought him. . . . I must seek him whom my soul loves" (3:1-2). A woman's desire to be with her husband—in ways that are healthy, not smothering—is one of the cords that ties a man to home and keeps him from wandering the neighborhood.

As she eagerly anticipated his return, she began to list all the things she loved about him: his hair, his eyes, his cheeks, his hands, and more.

Here, as throughout the Song of Solomon, you see the Shulammite's admiration of her husband and her expressed desire to be with him. This is what keeps a man at home, not just sex. Sex can be very mechanical, and if it is merely to find release for one's passions, then basically anyone will do.

But God intended the uniting of the two into one flesh to be so much more. It is an expression of gratitude, delight in the oneness of heart, mind, soul, and body. It is knowing, *This is bone of my bone, flesh of my flesh.* It is sealing the other upon your heart, possessing your possession, being able to delight the one who delights you, needs you, and wants you. It is the expression not just of love but also of friendship on the highest level. Marriage is an exclusive relationship, for this is where you will give yourself to one another in a way you will never share with any other.

Listen to what the Shulammite said of her husband to others: "His mouth is full of sweetness. And he is wholly desirable. This is my beloved and this is my friend, O daughters of Jerusalem" (5:16). Given how women are made, this comment may have more to do with how he talked to her than how he kissed her!

The man is commanded to love his wife with an *agape* love, a selfless love that desires another's highest good. But this love is commanded, something to be done regardless of how one feels. What all of us really long for is the love that brings delight to a marriage, the handholding, the winking, the "I'm looking forward to tonight" signals, the "I am my beloved's, and he is mine." This is the *phileo* love that makes marriage rich—the love of friendship, admiration, appreciation, and delight because of what you see in the other person or what he evokes in you because of who he is and how he treats you.

Nothing makes me want to draw closer to my husband than when he prays for me, when I hear him thank God for the things he sees, admires, and appreciates in me. The kindnesses, the compliments during the day make a woman want to say yes, to roll into her husband's arms rather than teetering on the edge of the bed for fear he'll get ideas. And when I admire Jack, when he feels good about himself, the whole mood around the house can change. The sun comes out, and the black clouds are blown away by the sweetness of my speech.

**What do you love and admire about your husband?
Do you tell him?**

Phileo is the love we long for—and this is the love and friendship you see in the Song of Solomon and why she called her husband "my friend." Put it into practice and watch what happens. See what it does to your sex life. Just remember, if you haven't expressed this kind of love in a long time, it might take your mate a long time to believe you are really sincere. But oh, when he is finally convinced, you will see things change in the living room as well as in the bedroom.

"And your mouth like the best wine! It goes down smoothly for my beloved, Flowing gently through the lips of those who fall asleep" (7:9). And we thought the wedding night was wonderful! (You did notice, didn't you, that she wasn't bundled up in flannel pajamas?) What you just read is the experience of love, of learning to know, appreciate, and delight one another. In Song of Solomon 7:6 we see that his wife was not only beautiful in his eyes but she was delightful to him. He loved her personality.

How I want to be delightful! Fun, interesting to be with. Joyful, not morbid. Positive, not negative. Building up, not tearing down. And what does this dear woman know without a shadow of a doubt? "I am my beloved's, and his desire is for me" (7:10).

Every woman needs to be assured that "his desire is for *me*." Do you remember what Solomon said on their wedding night? Twice he talked of her being "with me ... come with me." This is the beauty of sex according to God. Sex creates an oneness that goes far beyond the bedroom, a companionship we all need—but especially the man. Remember, woman was made because it was not good for the man to be alone.

And how did Solomon's wife respond to such love and passion? She planned an outing for them, a time to get away, a time to make love.

SONG OF SOLOMON 7:11-13

[11] "Come, my beloved, let us go out into the country,
   Let us spend the night in the villages.
[12] Let us rise early and go to the vineyards;
   Let us see whether the vine has budded
   And its blossoms have opened,
   And whether the pomegranates have bloomed.
   There I will give you my love.
[13] The mandrakes have given forth fragrance;
   And over our doors are all choice fruits,
   Both new and old,
   Which I have saved up for you, my beloved."

Mandrakes were believed to be an aphrodisiac. Jacob's wives bartered for them, and this wife had some delights in mind for her husband. What are they? It does not matter; they were for the two of them alone—beautiful and pleasing.

What message did this send to her husband? It affirmed his manhood; it nurtured him and built his confidence. When a man is down on himself—when it's rough at work and he's not appreciated, when he's laid off or loses his job—that's when he needs his wife the most in the bedroom. He longs to be assured that she needs him, wants him, believes in him, and delights in him. (See Eph. 5:33 about reverencing your husband.)

When a friend's husband lost his job and it took ages for him to find another, she made it a point of seeing that they made love frequently. It was her way of letting him know how special he was and how she needed him. It sustained him well. As a matter of fact, he later confided that it was her delight in him sexually that kept him from feeling like a failure as a man.

What about those who hop from one person's bed to another? They will never be satisfied, for sex according to God is so much more. What makes sex so beautiful is more than the act itself and its release of sexual tension. Rather, it is the whole giving of oneself to another. It is serving each other, ministering life and encouragement—and that's why a woman or a man doesn't want just another bed partner. It's not just the climax of the orgasm; it's the oneness that goes beyond the physical to touch spirit and soul.

The couple we meet in the Song of Solomon share a love that will never be violated, a covenant that will never be broken. This is the assurance he gave her.

SONG OF SOLOMON 8:6-7
⁶ "Put me like a seal over your heart,
   Like a seal on your arm.
   For love is as strong as death,
   Jealousy is as severe as Sheol;
   Its flashes are flashes of fire,
   The very flame of the LORD.
⁷ Many waters cannot quench love,
   Nor will rivers overflow it;
   If a man were to give all the riches of his house for love,
   It would be utterly despised."

These are words every bride longs to hear, the assurance we each seek, and the knowledge that on earth, as in heaven, there is one who will never leave us, never forsake us.

The seal was a mark of ownership. When two become one flesh, they are owned by each other for life "until death do us part." Such a couple has a divine jealousy even as God was jealous over Israel, a godly jealousy for those betrothed to Jesus Christ (see Ex. 34:14; 2 Cor. 11:2). Because this couple's relationship was so very beautiful, they wanted their little sister, who had not yet come to sexual maturity, to enjoy the same experience, the same intimacy when she found the one who would love her above all else.

Listen once again, dear single ones.

SONG OF SOLOMON 8:8-9
8 "We have a little sister,
   And she has no breasts;
   What shall we do for our sister
   On the day when she is spoken for?
9 If she is a wall,
   We will build on her a battlement of silver;
   But if she is a door,
   We will barricade her with planks of cedar."

They were going to protect her virginity—at all costs and with walls and barricades—so that if the time and opportunity ever came for her to marry, she too would experience the beauty of sex as God intended it. It was what the Shulammite maid experienced. "I was a wall, and my breasts were like towers; then I became in his eyes as one who finds peace" (8:10). Oh, the peace that comes when sex is according to God.

As you read this you may be saddened, grieved because you believe you'll never experience the beauty of sex. You may be thinking, *Why should I care whether or not sex is beautiful? I know I'll never marry.*

My friend, Jesus, knows exactly what you're facing. Jesus was the virgin of virgins when it came to sexual purity. He lived over 30 years and never knew what it was to touch a woman. Yet He was cut off in the prime of life for everyone who had been immoral, "He was cut off and had nothing" (Dan. 9:26). However, in His selflessness and sacrifice He gained a bride—and soon He will come for her and take her home. Then each of us who is part of the body of Jesus Christ, the church, will know the beauty of a oneness, a union of unions hitherto inexperienced.

Single or married, widowed or divorced, pure or desecrated—a day of inexplicable beauty, wordless joy, and absolute fulfillment is coming for each and every one of God's children. It is called the marriage supper of the Lamb. You may not have your heart's desire on earth, but you will in heaven! Heaven is for eternity. No wonder they shout, "Hallelujah! For the Lord God omnipotent reigns" (Rev. 19:6-9).

DAY FOUR

COULD GOD EVER FORGIVE *ME?*

What do you do when what you have done or what someone has done to you has violated the Word of God? Is there any hope for forgiveness with God, restoration, healing—wholeness? And what about the perpetrator—what do you do about what that person did to you? Getting God's answers to these questions and then dealing with the situation according to God's precepts is the answer, beloved. From all I know about God in His Word, healing and redemption follow *if* you will seek it God's way.

First of all, let's look at how we deal with our transgressions. To transgress is to break God's commandment, to go over the line He has drawn. Even if you are not aware of His law, it is still sin and sin brings God's judgment.

Let's reason together. Think this through because the key that unlocks the door to healing and hope is the mind—thinking truth, believing it, and ordering your life accordingly. I am going to ask you to do several things. If you will do them, I believe you will know and experience not only the forgiveness of God but also the sweet peace and relief that comes from knowing absolutely everything is taken care of between you and God—you're at peace.

And what if you have taken care of everything in a biblical way and are already at peace with God? Don't close the book or skip today's lesson. Many who are in terrible straits are hurting unbelievably. They desperately need to know what to do and that hope exists in God.

Now, beloved, you are going to do some personal writing. You may use a separate piece of paper and destroy it when finished, for you will be totally clean, forgiven by God.

- What did you do you that went over the line and broke God's law? Write it out, naming the sin for what it was. Then read what you wrote out loud to God.

- Do you acknowledge that what you did was an offense against God? If so, write it out and ask God to forgive you. Tell Him that you have sinned against Him and that you are very sorry—not because you got caught but because you grieved His holiness and transgressed His righteousness. Read your words aloud.

First John 1:9–2:2 was written to children of God. Read the verses aloud and mark the following:
- every reference to *sin* (color it brown)
- every reference to "we," including related pronouns such as *us* and *you* (color it orange)
- every reference to God—you can use yellow or a triangle
- Mark the reference to Jesus, including the pronouns that relate to Him, differently than the way you mark *God.* You could use a cross.

1 JOHN 1:9-10
⁹ If we confess our sins, He is faithful and righteous to forgive us our sins and to cleanse us from all unrighteousness.
¹⁰ If we say that we have not sinned, we make Him a liar and His word is not in us.

I JOHN 2:1-2

1 My little children, I am writing these things to you so that you may not sin. And if anyone sins, we have an Advocate with the Father, Jesus Christ the righteous;

2 and He Himself is the propitiation for our sins; and not for ours only, but also for those of the whole world.

(*Propitiation* means Jesus' offering of His blood, His life for your life, thus satisfying the holiness and justice of God.)

Now list in the appropriate columns what you learned from marking the following:

WE/US	GOD	JESUS CHRIST

According to the verses you just marked and your confession of sin before that, what has happened to you?

Now, look at Psalm 32:1-5, a psalm of David. Read it and mark these things:

- He and every other pronoun that goes with the first "he." Include the "I" and other pronouns that refer to David such as "my." Also mark "man" and "whose" in the last verse.
- Every reference to *sin, transgression,* and *iniquity.*
- Every reference to God.

PSALM 32:1-5

¹ How blessed is he whose transgression is forgiven,
   Whose sin is covered!
² How blessed is the man to whom the LORD
   does not impute iniquity,
   (Impute means to put to someone's account. To charge as a debit)
   And in whose spirit there is no deceit!
³ When I kept silent about my sin, my body wasted away
   Through my groaning all day long.
⁴ For day and night Your hand was heavy upon me;
   My vitality was drained away as with the fever heat
   of summer.
⁵ I acknowledged my sin to You,
   And my iniquity I did not hide;
   I said, "I will confess my transgressions to the LORD";
   And You forgave the guilt of my sin.

List what you learned from marking:

| THE MAN/ | SIN/INIQUITY | THE LORD |
| DAVID | TRANSGRESSION | |

Now, faithful one, open your Bible and read Psalm 51. Ask God to speak to your heart and to help you understand and experience the truths of this psalm. Note at the beginning who wrote it and when. Then, if you are willing to mark your Bible, mark the text as you've marked the Scriptures today. When you finish, express your heart to God in regard to all you have done today. Write out your prayer if you like.

SING A NEW SONG
TO THE LORD

Isn't it wonderful to know you are forgiven—to know that God cannot lie, will not lie, that His Word is true and that you are right with God because you obeyed Him in faith? Now, beloved, every emotion, every thought, every feeling must be brought into obedience to what has taken place. The enemy would love to whisper a lie to you—to tell you that God didn't hear, that you weren't sincere, or whatever lie pushes your panic/doubt button. But do not listen. Instead, you *must* believe God.

Remember, the battle is for your mind. Therefore, you are to "bring every thought captive to the obedience of Jesus Christ." No imagining what if's, if only's, or I don't feel's. Just reality. God has forgiven you and cleansed you from all unrighteousness. The blood of Jesus Christ has cleansed you from all sin. When your mind starts to panic or doubt, simply stop and thank God for what He has done. Sing a new song to the Lord; make melody in your heart to the Lord.

If you are thinking, *But I cannot forgive myself*—put those thoughts away. Who are you, the one who chose to do what you did, to forgive yourself? It is against God and God alone that you have sinned, and He has forgiven you. It is done (Ps. 51:3-4,6-7). Walk in faith and please God by thanking and praising Him for loving you so very much that He would give His Son to die for your sins so that you might have Jesus' righteousness (2 Cor. 5:21).

Now, what are you to do *after* adultery, fornication, or sexual abuse? How do you relate to the person you "defrauded" (I Thess. 4:6)? What should you do after committing an immoral act with another person? We'll talk about those who abused you in a moment, but do this first.

Read Matthew 5:23-24 carefully. Mark *you* in one way and *the brother* in another.

MATTHEW 5:23-24

[23] "Therefore if you are presenting your offering at the altar, and there remember that your brother has something against you,

[24] leave your offering there before the altar and go; first be reconciled to your brother, and then come and present your offering.

What did you learn from marking the text?
Write your insights below.

If you have been sexually involved with someone in any way, then "your brother or your sister" has something against you, especially if you were the aggressor or more than a willing participant. Consequently, you must go to the person if at all possible or call or write and take responsibility for your sin.

You must confess what you have done. Talk about it with no other, but go to the person and name your sin for what it is; do not downplay the gravity of what you have done. God tells us if we cover our sins we will not prosper, but if we confess and forsake them we will find mercy. Hopefully mercy will come from the offended one, but most certainly from God—and therein lies your strength.

We see in Psalm 51 that confessing your sin to God will prepare you to deal with others and with the consequences of your sin—whatever they are. However, if you don't have God's absolution through your confession to Him as I John 1:9 says, then you have no foundation on which to build any other relationship. Remember, "against You, You only, I have sinned" (Ps. 51:4).

If your sin was committed against a child or constituted rape, then you must pay the consequences. You cannot expect to go free, nor should you. King David took his fourfold punishment like a man, never complaining. Take your sentence as from God and use your circumstances to become the woman God would have you be from that day forward. God grants forgiveness, but this does not negate the consequences of your sin.

If you have committed adultery you have ...

    broken God's commandment and a covenant agreement

    put your marriage and your mate at risk

    jeopardized your children's future and failed them
      as a role model

    sinned against your own body

    defrauded another person and caused him to come
      under God's judgment

    sinned against the church, and against the community

You have done something worthy of death under Old Testament law. This cannot be treated lightly and brushed aside with an "I'm sorry." You must take stock of the enormity of your sexual transgression and treat it accordingly.

SEEK GOD AND GIVE HIM TIME TO WORK

What about confessing to your mate? This is where I would tell you to seek God diligently and do what He specifically lays on your heart. He knows how your mate will handle it. Some men can't get over it or get it out of their minds. And if they are not children of God, they do not have the Spirit of God to help them—although God may use this circumstance to bring your husband to Him. Remember, Proverbs 6:34-35 tells us that "jealousy enrages a man, and he will not spare in the day of vengeance. He will not accept any ransom (nothing will appease him) nor will he be satisfied though you give many gifts."

Do I personally advise you always confess to God? Absolutely. Nothing will be right until you do. To your mate? No, not always. This answer gets me in trouble with some individuals. You may feel really angry with me right now, and I understand; but I must be true to my heart and what I know about the Word of God. Therefore, I am leaving this important issue between you and God. If you want God's will, He will make it plain—just give Him time to show you and don't open your mouth until He does.

If you choose to confess, make sure you take into account your sin's grievousness. Also be sure that your heart is broken and your spirit is contrite, just as you read in Psalm 51. Then confess what you have done, name it for what it is, and agree with God that it is worthy of death. Don't go into details (your spouse doesn't need any picture in his mind to torment him), don't excuse yourself, and don't place the blame anywhere but on yourself. Be sure you come to him in godly sorrow and genuine repentance. Be willing to do whatever is necessary within the bounds of Scripture to heal the situation. When you do this, beloved, you can expect things to be different.

Give God time to heal your relationship. Let this healing time deepen your relationship with God. In Hosea 3, after Hosea bought back his harlot wife and took her home, he didn't go to her as his wife for a while. He first gave them a time of healing, a time to show and express love apart from sex. Then the time came to come together as one flesh, to promise fidelity from that point on.

What if your mate will not take you back? Whether or not your mate forgives and is willing to restore your relationship, you must fill your life with God. When you fill your life with God and give God time, there is yet hope of restoration and a stronger foundation for restructuring your marriage.

WHAT IF YOU'VE BEEN SEXUALLY ABUSED?

Perhaps you've been misused sexually—abused, raped, betrayed. What do you do when the sexual transgression has been against you? Then, beloved, you have a choice to make!

You can be bitter or angry. You can rage, hate, or seek revenge. Yet none of these will ever take care of the person's sin against you. Instead of punishing the perpetrator, you will punish only yourself and once again become the victim. If you choose instead to handle it God's way, you will know a healing and a freedom you thought you never would experience again.

Of course, we need to talk about recovering from the trauma of what was done to us sexually. If this situation pertains to you, how do you handle someone who has abused or misused you sexually? If you want to be free, you need to forgive. Otherwise you will find yourself in a prison of pain, remorse, and bitterness with your perpetrator as guard.

FREE TO FORGIVE

When the apostle Peter asked Jesus how many times he was to forgive his brother, Jesus responded, "Up to seventy times seven" (Matt. 18:22). Quick math—490 times. You'd surely lose count! Jesus then followed with an explanation to Peter about the kingdom of heaven. Remember, if you pray according to the Lord's Prayer, your prayer is that His kingdom (not yours) would come and that God's will would be done on earth as it is in heaven. What, then, is His will in respect to you and your perpetrator?

> **Read what Jesus said in Matthew 18:23-30 and mark the following in a distinctive way. I'll give you some ideas.**
> - Debt (owed, mark with a $)
> - Forgiven (mark with a ✝)
> - Slave (first one mentioned with the 10,000-talent debt, equal to about 15 years wages as a laborer; use brown)
> - Slave number two—the one who owes 100 denarii (A denarius was a day's wage. Mark in red.)
> - The lord of the slaves (Use yellow or triangle.)
> - Also watch for the words "felt compassion," "mercy," "heart." You could use a ♡ for all of these words.

MATTHEW 18:23-35

23 For this reason the kingdom of heaven may be compared
   to a king who wished to settle accounts with his slaves.
24 When he had begun to settle them, one who owed him
   ten thousand talents was brought to him.

²⁵ But since he did not have the means to repay, his lord commanded him to be sold, along with his wife and children and all that he had, and repayment to be made.

²⁶ So the slave fell to the ground and prostrated himself before him, saying, "Have patience with me and I will repay you everything."

²⁷ And the lord of that slave felt compassion and released him and forgave him the debt.

²⁸ But that slave went out and found one of his fellow slaves who owed him a hundred denarii; and he seized him and began to choke him, saying, "Pay back what you owe."

²⁹ So his fellow slave fell to the ground and began to plead with him, saying, "Have patience with me and I will repay you."

³⁰ But he was unwilling and went and threw him in prison until he should pay back what was owed.

³¹ So when his fellow slaves saw what had happened, they were deeply grieved and came and reported to their lord all that had happened.

³² Then summoning him, his lord said to him, "You wicked slave, I forgave you all that debt because you pleaded with me.

³³ Should you not also have had mercy on your fellow slave, in the same way that I had mercy on you?"

³⁴ And his lord, moved with anger, handed him over to the torturers until he should repay all that was owed him.

³⁵ My heavenly Father will also do the same to you, if each of you does not forgive his brother from your heart.

List the insights you gained from your markings.

SLAVE #1	SLAVE #2	THE LORD OF THE SLAVES

What do you learn from marking *forgive* and *forgave?*

In your own Bible read Matthew 6:14-15 and answer:
What is the teaching of these verses?
How do these verses compare with Matthew 18?

What do you learn in Matthew 18 from the occurrences of compassion and mercy?

Are you willing to be merciful to the person who sexually abused or misused you? Give the reason for your answer.

What is the bottom line of the story according to Jesus in Matthew 18:35? As you answer this question, explain what you think Jesus meant when He said "from your heart."

When I mention forgiving the perpetrator of your pain, I know you may feel like shaking your head and saying, "Never! Never in a thousand years!" I understand.; I have grieved with too many women. However, please know that forgiving does not mean the offender goes free and escapes God's just judgment. When you forgive as God in Christ Jesus has forgiven you, then you remove yourself from the role of judge and executioner for which you are not suited anyway.

God's role as Judge and Executioner is for those who will never bow the knee to Him and allow Him to take control of their lives. Believe me, God will do His part. His righteousness demands it. While you say you could never forgive them in a thousand years, God says they shall suffer forever. Read Revelation 20:11-15; Isaiah 66:22-24; and 2 Thessalonians 1:6-10 with the emphasis on Isaiah 66:24. These tell of the days when God's wrath is poured out on the unbelieving, the unrepentant.

God will wipe away your tears, while they will never cease to cry, "Why? Why didn't I believe?" To forgive is to give up your right to punish. Your forgiveness annuls every excuse your perpetrator gives you for his sin. Now he is face-to-face with God, for you have just demon-strated God to him by your response.

You also need to understand that to forgive does not mean that you must act as if that person never violated you. You are to love your enemy, to extend God's *agape* love that desires his highest good—that the viola-tor might be saved. However, you do not need to hang around with him or demonstrate affection to him. God loves the world and sacrificed His Son for all mankind, but it does not guarantee the world a relationship with God. Jesus loved the rich young ruler, but He let him walk away because the man preferred riches to the kingdom of God.

If your violator or covenant breaker does not confess his sin and ask your forgiveness, there can be neither relationship nor a valid reason for one. This is obvious in Scripture. No one can have fellowship with God or share anything in common with Him until there is an acknowledg-ment of sin, a verbal agreement that what was done was wrong.

First John 1 makes this clear. Read verses 4-10 and mark
sin **with a big S and** *fellowship* **with a symbol like this :** ⏝.
Fellowship **means to share in common, like two fellows in one**
boat (ship). This will help you see what I am saying.

I JOHN 1:4-10
⁴ These things we write, so that our joy may be made
complete.
⁵ This is the message we have heard from Him and announce
to you, that God is Light, and in Him there is no darkness
at all.
⁶ If we say that we have fellowship with Him and yet walk
in the darkness, we lie and do not practice the truth;
⁷ but if we walk in the Light as He Himself is in the Light,
we have fellowship with one another, and the blood of
Jesus His Son cleanses us from all sin.
⁸ If we say that we have no sin, we are deceiving ourselves
and the truth is not in us.

⁹ If we confess our sins, He is faithful and righteous to forgive
us our sins and to cleanse us from all unrighteousness.

¹⁰ If we say that we have not sinned, we make Him a liar and
His word is not in us.

Can you see how imperative it is that sin be recognized and confessed as such? God says that those who cover their sins will never prosper. Without confession there will be no healing. Therefore, it is crucial that sin be brought out in the open and dealt with accordingly.

ALL THINGS BECOME LIGHT

When men or women get away with immorality, they will only continue to misuse God's gift of sex and seduce others to do evil. Surely by now you realize that sex apart from marriage is sin. Sin is evil, and it belongs to the kingdom of darkness. Ephesians 5 says that all things become light when they are exposed. As you study the whole Word of God and get to know and understand His ways, these things will become increasingly clear and give you firm direction for your life.

A woman who had been sexually molested by her father when she was a child demonstrates beautifully the power of God's Word when it is studied and obeyed:

> From the day I walked into my first Precept study, the Holy Spirit began to convict me of things in my life that were not like Him. Some of those things remained in my life as a direct result of my ignorance. Some things lingered on because I yet had unforgiveness, hatred, anger, and bitterness in my heart.
>
> My father sexually molested me when I was a young girl, and I made it my business to make him pay for what he had done to me. I made sure he knew I hated him, and I did not respect or honor him as my father. I felt I had a right to be treated with kindness and love, so I made it my business to right the wrong my dad had

done. But I learned that I had no rights except to serve God and then that isn't a right but a privilege.

I realized I would be forgiven only to the extent I forgave others. I recognized that I was to love as God loved me: unconditionally and unselfishly. Love was an act of my will. I chose to love and expect nothing back in return.

I asked Dad to forgive me for my wrong attitude and actions toward him, and I began to honor him and share the gospel with him, as I didn't want him to spend eternity in hell. One day we were talking and God revealed my dad's heart to me. I began to tell him things only God could have made known to me, and my heart was overwhelmed with love and compassion for him only God could give.

I remember my dad's words to this day, "I know there is a God, because you of all people have forgiven me." My dad sobbed loudly over the telephone, and I felt a wall between us come tumbling down. ...

Kay, who truly knows the heart? Only our One and True God. I continue to witness to my dad long distance, and I see God cleansing and drawing him into His arms. I continue to thank God and stand firm.

This is what salvation is all about: the kingdom of heaven and forgiveness of sins. When we don't forgive, then according to Jesus we are turned over to the torturers (see Matt. 18:23-25). You only damage yourself.

If you are tortured because of sexual immorality, then seek God's forgiveness today. It will become a day of days, I promise! Then begin the process of forgiving even as God has forgiven you. The peace and release it will bring cannot be bought—except by the Lamb of God who takes away the sins of the world. "It is a trustworthy statement, deserving full acceptance, that Christ Jesus came into the world to save sinners, among whom I am foremost of all" (1 Tim. 1:15).

VIEWER GUIDE
SESSION 6

THE WAY LOVE SHOULD BE

There is _____ and it comes through the Word of God.

God has brought this message to you at the _____ He wants you to have it.

Romans 12:1:
"Therefore I urge you, brethren, by the mercies of God, to present your bodies a living and holy sacrifice, acceptable to God, which is your spiritual service of worship."

Do not let the world _____ you into its mold.

Charge: Live not for yourself but for God.

ENDNOTES

WEEK 1

1. R. L. Harris, G. L., Archer, B. K. Waltke. *Theological Wordbook of the Old Testament* (electronic ed.) (550). Chicago: Moody Press.
2. For more information on Precept Upon Precept courses, In & Out studies, and 40-Minute studies such as *Building a Marriage That Lasts*, go to *www.precept.org* or call 1-800-763-1990. *A Marriage Without Regrets* is available at LifeWay stores and other Christian book stores.
3. Understanding what it means to be in covenant with God is life changing. *Our Covenant God* is available at LifeWay stores and other Christian book stores or by calling 1-800-763-1990.
4. Read an allegory in an evening: *With An Everlasting Love* tells this story of God's love for you.

WEEK 2

1. Matthew 1:18-25 tells us that Mary, a virgin, was engaged to Joseph when the angel told her she would conceive and give birth to the Son of God. When Joseph found out she was with child, he decided to divorce her, thus absolving him from the covenant agreement.
2. Spiros Zodhiates, gen. ed., *The Complete Word Study Dictionary: New Testament* (Chattanooga, TN: AMG Publishers, 1992), 1202.
3. Ibid., 940.
4. Ibid., 258.
5. J. Swanson (1997). *Dictionary of Biblical Languages with Semantic Domains: Hebrew (Old Testament)* (electronic ed.) (HGK2773). Oak Harbor: Logos Research Systems, Inc.

WEEK 3

1. Dawn Herzog Jewell, "Red-Light Rescue," *Christianity Today*, January 2007, 29.
2. Ibid., 32.
3. Ibid., 30.
4. God has used powerfully *Lord, Heal My Hurts*. Check *www.precept.org* or Christian stores.
5. Doris VanStone with Erwin W. Lutzer. *Dorie: The Girl Nobody Loved* (Chicago: Moody Press, 1979).
6. Doris VanStone and Erwin W. Lutzer. *No Place to Cry: The Hurt and Healing of Sexual Abuse* (Chicago: Moody Press, 1992).
7. R. L. Harris, G. L. Archer, & B. K. Waltke (1999, c1980). *Theological Wordbook of the Old Testament* (electronic ed.) (161) (Chicago: Moody Press).
8. Jay Rogers. "Mass Murder and Pornography on the University of Florida Campus," *The Forerunner* [online], Sept. 1990 [retrieved 6 November 2007]. Available at: *www.forerunner.com*.

WEEK 4

1. Bob Reccord, *Beneath the Surface* (Nashville: Broadman and Holman, 2002), 73-75.
2. PT Leena, "The ABCs of STDs: Information on Risks, Symptoms and Statistics," Assoc. Content [online], 2007 [retrieved 19 Oct. 2007]. Available at: *www.associatedcontent.com*.
3. Spiros Zodhiates, gen. ed., *The Complete Word Study Dictionary: New Testament* (Chattanooga, TN: AMG Publishers, 1992), 1202.
4. Stephen Arterbaurn and Fred Stoeker with Mike Yorkey. *Every Man's Battle: Winning the War on Sexual Temptation One Victory at a Time* (Colorado Springs: WaterBrook Press, 2000), 13-14.

WEEK 5

1. Adapted from *The Truth About Sex* (Colorado Springs: WaterBrook Press, 2002), 193.
2. Sallie Foley, Sally Kope, Dennis Sugrue. *Sex Matters for Women* (New York: Guilford Publications, 2002).

This leader guide will help you facilitate six 1½-hour group sessions. If you have the Leader Kit (Item 005035532), use the DVDs. If you do not have the kit, you may prefer to omit the introductory session (I), having participants complete the week I home study before your first session.

Each session has a suggestion to create interest in the discussion and several questions to help women discuss the week's material before viewing Kay's video. Afterward, provide a brief time for ladies to make personal application of God's principles. Begin and end each session with prayer! Additional help is available online (*www.lifeway.com/women*).

LEADING A DISCUSSION GROUP

You don't need to be a gifted teacher or a sex therapist to lead these small groups. You do need a firm belief in God's Word as the complete guide and authority for life; compassion and desire for women to embrace God's design for sexuality; a TV and DVD player; and a meeting place.

Prayerfully determine the group's composition. Will it be made up of married women? single women? a combination? mothers and daughters? The participants will determine the group dynamics and discussion. Promote the study in the church newsletter, worship bulletin, bulletin boards, and, most effectively, through personal invitation.

Before each session complete each week's assignments prayerfully. The most effective way to lead is to allow God's Word to transform you and then let that transformation overflow to the women in your small group. Adapt the leader guide suggestions for each session as needed.

Evaluate each session: *What exercises either encouraged or squelched discussion? Do you need to direct questions to keep one person from monopolizing the discussion? Would discussion in groups of two or three encourage quieter women to speak up?* Pray for each participant by name and ask God to guide each session.

KNOWLEDGE
OF GOD IN THE LAND

BEFORE THE SESSION

1. Have copies of *Return to the Garden* ready for distribution. (To order this resource: write to LifeWay Church Resources Customer Service; One LifeWay Plaza; Nashville, TN 37234-0013; fax (615) 251-5933; phone toll-free (800) 458-2772; order online at *www.lifeway.com*; e-mail *orderentry@lifeway.com*; or visit the LifeWay Christian Store serving you.)

2. Prepare an attendance sheet for participants. Include a space for e-mail addresses in the information you request. Place it on a table near the door along with pens, markers, and name tags. Ask women to sign the attendance sheet as they arrive.

3. In advance, cue the DVD to session 1 video.

4. Make a copy of the "How Does Your Garden Grow?" (p. 185) icebreaker activity for each participant.

DURING THE SESSION

1. As women arrive ask them to sign in, prepare name tags, and pick up their books. You may have a few still deciding whether to participate.

2. After women sign in give them a copy of "How Does Your Garden Grow?" and direct them to ask the questions of other women in the group. After everyone has had time to mingle, ask each participant to introduce another woman in the group by sharing what she discovered about that woman's gardening preferences.

3. Use "About the Author" (p. 5) and "About This Study" (p. 8) to introduce Kay Arthur and this study.

4. Make certain women know this is a Bible study concerning sexuality and not gardening! Ask: *How is sex in our culture really "in your face"? How does this world's in-your-face sexual assault cause women to feel about themselves and their intimate relationships?*

Remark that *Return to the Garden* is an in-your-face study about *God's* plan for sexuality. Request that the group scan the Contents page. Explore together how this study can lead women to feel about themselves and their intimate relationships based on what God's Word has to say about this important subject.

5. Ask ladies to leaf through week 1 (pp. 10-33) and to note the five-day format and learning activities. Use "Discovering God's Truth for Yourself" on pages 6-7 to explain Kay's inductive approach to Bible study.

Encourage the women to purchase a variety of colored highlighters or pencils for this study. Urge them to study daily and to complete every activity in order to get the most out of this study.

6. Explain that each small-group session will provide time for a discussion of what ladies learned in their own personal study. Remind members that everything said in the group sessions will remain confidential.

7. Request women turn to the viewer guide on page 9 and take notes as they watch the video. Play the session 1 video.

8. Ask ladies to write their personal goals for this study at the bottom of their viewer guide.

9. Close in prayer, asking God to accomplish the women's goals, Kay's goals, but most importantly His goals for this study. Pray for the ladies' dedication, ability, and time to complete each week's study.

How Does Your GARDEN GROW?

Ask each woman a different question from this list. (If there are more than 12 women, you'll need to ask a question twice.) Be sure to record the name of the woman who answered the question.

Do you have a garden? What do you grow?　Name _____

What's your favorite flower?　Name _____

What's your favorite fruit?　Name _____

What's your favorite vegetable?　Name _____

Do you have a brown or green thumb?
Give an example.　Name _____

Do you love or hate gardening? Why?　Name _____

What's your favorite activity in a garden?　Name _____

Have you ever visited a famous garden?
Which one?　Name _____

What is the most beautiful garden you
have ever seen? Describe it.　Name _____

What is your greatest gardening triumph?　Name _____

What is your worst gardening disaster?　Name _____

Describe your dream garden.　Name _____

THE BEAUTY OF
A WOMAN'S
SEXUALITY

In advance, cue the DVD to session 2.

DURING THE SESSION

1. Ask ladies to rank on a scale of 1 to 10 (1 = extremely uncomfortable, 10 = extremely comfortable) how they feel about discussing sex in a Bible study. Discuss from page 13 where our sexuality is usually discussed. State: *Our group is going to discuss sexuality in a safe, godly environment with God's Word as the guide.*

2. Lead ladies to discuss these questions (if necessary, choose to fit your time frame/audience):
   • Summarize what you learned about your sexuality from
     1 Thessalonians 4:1-8.
   • What do you love about being a woman? What makes us
     distinctively and delightfully female?
   • How did your first lesson on sex compare with Kay's?
     How can we give our children that gift of a positive first lesson?
     (Note: In our day you can't wait until they are 12!)
   • What lessons about your body and sex did you gain from
     1 Corinthians 6:15-20?
   • What did God design sex to be? What is true intimacy?
   • As you consider the divine romance between Christ and the
     church, why must women make it their goal to be pure?

3. Request women turn to the viewer guide on page 33 and take notes as they watch the video. Play the session 2 video.

4. Give ladies time to complete in writing what they need to do in light of what they've learned this week (p. 32). Urge women who have never accepted Christ as their Savior to make that their priority application. Offer to speak with them after the session. Close in prayer.

THE GIFT YOU CAN ONLY GIVE ONCE

BEFORE THE SESSION

1. Cue the DVD to session 3.
2. Purchase Nestles Treasures®.

DURING THE SESSION

1. Ask: *What is the gift we can only give once?* Guide the group to describe society's attitude toward virginity, using examples from music, movies, and magazines. Acknowledge that Kay led you to look at some difficult passages this week. Remind the ladies that God's Word, though convicting, is always redemptive and for our good.

2. Lead women to discuss (choose to fit your time frame/audience):
   • Why must we know God's Word?
   • What did you learn about virginity from Deuteronomy 22:13-21?
   • What did you learn from Deuteronomy 22:22-29 and Exodus 22:16-17 about whom and what God protects and values?
   • How could obeying God's command to set ourselves apart change the church and impact our society?
   • How does sexual immorality still result in death? So is there any such thing as safe sex? Explain your answer.
   • What's the relationship between morality and self-control in I Corinthians 7?

3. Request women turn to the viewer guide on page 67 and take notes as they watch the video. Play the session 3 video.

4. Discuss: *What is a pure virgin? How can any woman feel like a virgin again?*

5. Give a Nestles Treasures® to each woman. Declare: *No matter what you've done or what has been done to you, you are God's treasure.* Urge participants who are still virgins to commit to protect their treasure until they are married and those who are married to preserve their treasure for their husbands alone. Close in prayer.

MAN: PREDATOR OR PROTECTOR?

In advance cue the DVD to session 4.

DURING THE SESSION

1. Ask: *How did your list of qualities you want in a husband change as you matured? What is at the top of your list of qualities for an ideal husband now?*

2. Lead the ladies to discuss (choose to fit your time frame/audience):
   - How does culture allow, even encourage, men to be predators?
   - *I see man as a _____ in Genesis 2:21-25 because . . .*
   - How did the woman see herself in respect to the man and why?
   - What did you observe about the role of man from Ephesians 5? What parallels did you make with Genesis 2?
   - How can we teach boys and young men under our influence about a man's true role toward women?
   - How should wives behave toward their husbands regardless of how well their men are living out Ephesians 5? Why?
   - What is the purpose of the God-rules in Leviticus 18 and 20?
   - What cautions do mothers gain from Amnon and Tamar's story? What safeguards must we have for our children and ourselves?
   - What hope is there for the Tamars of the world? (See 3 truths concluding day 1, p. 74.)

3. Request women turn to the viewer guide on page 101 and take notes as they watch the video. Play the session 4 video.

4. Organize women into marrieds and singles (single women with daughters might rather join the married women) and direct them to discuss:
   - (*Marrieds*): *How can we be our sisters' and daughters' keepers? What qualities in a man are we to teach our daughters to look for? How can we do that?*
   - (*Singles*): *How can we be our sisters' keepers? What qualities in a man are we to look for? What do we do if that kind of man is hard to find?*

5. Use Kay's directions at the end of day 1 to guide your prayer.

THE SEDUCTRESS
(AND HOW NOT TO BE ONE)

In advance cue the DVD to session 5.

DURING THE SESSION

1. State: *When it comes to seduction, the "eyes" have it. But we don't want to have it! We should desire purity instead.*

2. Discuss these questions:
   - Why do women act the seductress? How must we respond?
   - What did you learn about the seductress from Proverbs 5?
   - How can these Proverbs passages make us more aware of how we present ourselves? How can we be attractive but not seductive?

3. Organize women into marrieds and singles, allowing them to choose the group that best fits their circumstances. Ask them to discuss:
   - (*Marrieds*): How can we protect our husbands against seductresses without sounding like jealous shrews? How can we raise smart sons? What do we need to be watching for and curtailing in our daughters? What are some hard decisions we might have to make for our kids, and how can we help them understand?
   - (*Singles*): Why or why is it not OK to flirt? What's the difference between seeking a husband and being on the prowl? How can a godly girl get a guy with all the aggressive women "out there"?

4. Request women turn to the viewer guide on page 137 and take notes as they watch the video. Play the session 5 video.

5. Request women prayerfully consider the following questions and write their responses in the space at the conclusion of day 5:
   - What kind of covenant do you need to make with God about how you will relate with men?
   - Think through your wardrobe. What items need to be tossed?
   - What needs to be added or taken away from your eyes?

6. Close in prayer asking God to make us aware of how we dress.

THE WAY LOVE SHOULD BE

In advance cue DVD to session 6.

DURING THE SESSION

1. Read aloud Genesis 1:15,22 and Song of Solomon 4:12,16. Ask: *Now that we have completed our last week of study, what do you think is the meaning of the title,* Return to the Garden?

2. Ask the ladies what godly, biblical advice they would give to:
   a. a single woman who desperately wants to be loved by a man
   b. an engaged woman
   c. a married woman who feels ignored and unvalued by her husband
   d. a woman who has behaved immorally
   e. a woman who has been sexually violated
   f. a married woman who desires an ever-deepening and fulfilling relationship with her husband

3. Request women turn to the viewer guide on page 180 and take notes as they watch the video. Play the session 6 video.

4. Ask ladies to consider silently: *By the grace of God, how are you going to return to the garden and embrace God's design for your sexuality?*

5. Invite volunteers to share:
   • What commitment have you made that this group can pray about with you?
   • What issues are you still struggling with that we can pray about with you? (Even if ladies don't want to verbally share, urge them to write their commitment or struggles in their workbook as their own personal reminder.)

6. Allow women to pray for one another's commitments and struggles. Close in prayer.

A BOLD AND LIBERATING RESPONSE TO THE WORLD'S LIES ABOUT SEX

"Kay Arthur speaks healing truth to the most intimate wounds of our lives, and breathes beauty back to the places defiled by perversion and shame, answering every question we bring. This book is a gift."
—**Lisa Bevere,** best-selling author, *Kissed the Girls and Made Them Cry* and *Fight Like a Girl*

KAY ARTHUR
Best-Selling & Award-Winning Author

THE TRUTH ABOUT SEX

Foreword by
Hayley DiMarco,
best-selling author of *Dateable*

Previously released as *Sex...According to God*

With persuasive insights, practical applications, and thought-provoking questions, trusted author and Bible teacher Kay Arthur guides readers through a compelling, interactive study that explores God's design for sex and reveals the insidiously dangerous lies that permeate the culture. Includes a study guide suitable for individual or group use.

"Can a book about sex convict you and at the same time liberate you? Can it instruct you while encouraging you? Can it help you contain your thought life while increasing your imagination for sex with your husband? Can it help you resolve your past and usher you into a future with deeper and richer levels of intimacy? *The Truth About Sex* does all of that and more."

—Stephen Arterburn, best-selling co-author of the Every Man series

"When we understand the origins of sex and the reason for its existence, then we can begin to comprehend the beauty of its very nature and break free from the guilt so often associated with it."

—from the foreword by Hayley DiMarco, author of *Dateable* and *Mean Girls*

WATERBROOK PRESS
www.waterbrookpress.com

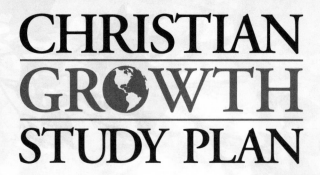

CHRISTIAN GROWTH STUDY PLAN

In the **Christian Growth Study Plan (formerly Church Study Course)**, this book RETURN TO THE GARDEN is a resource for course credit in the subject area BIBLE STUDIES of the Christian Growth category of plans. To receive credit, read the book, complete the learning activities, show your work to your pastor, a staff member or church leader, then complete the following information. This page may be duplicated. Send the completed page to:

Christian Growth Study Plan
One LifeWay Plaza
Nashville, TN 37234-0117
FAX: (615)251-5067
Email: cgspnet@lifeway.com

For information about the Christian Growth Study Plan, refer to the Christian Growth Study Plan Catalog. It is located online at www.lifeway.com/cgsp. If you do not have access to the Internet, contact the Christian Growth Study Plan office (1.800.968.5519) for the specific plan you need for your ministry.

RETURN TO THE GARDEN
COURSE NUMBER: CG-1330

PARTICIPANT INFORMATION

Social Security Number (USA ONLY-optional)	Personal CGSP Number*		Date of Birth (MONTH, DAY, YEAR)

Name (First, Middle, Last)		Home Phone

Address (Street, Route, or P.O. Box)	City, State, or Province	Zip/Postal Code

Email Address for CGSP use

Please check appropriate box: ❑ Resource purchased by church ❑ Resource purchased by self ❑ Other

CHURCH INFORMATION

Church Name

Address (Street, Route, or P.O. Box)	City, State, or Province	Zip/Postal Code

CHANGE REQUEST ONLY

☐ Former Name

☐ Former Address	City, State, or Province	Zip/Postal Code

☐ Former Church	City, State, or Province	Zip/Postal Code

Signature of Pastor, Conference Leader, or Other Church Leader	Date

*New participants are requested but not required to give SS# and date of birth. Existing participants, please give CGSP# when using SS# for the first time. Thereafter, only one ID# is required. **Mail to:** Christian Growth Study Plan, One LifeWay Plaza, Nashville, TN 37234-0117. Fax: (615)251-5067.

Revised 4-05